THE TRAVELLER'S HEALTHBOOK

THE TRAVELLER'S HEALTHBOOK

Edited by
Miranda Haines and Sarah Thorowgood

A  Publication

First Published in London in 1998
by WEXAS International
45-49 Brompton Road, London, SW3 1DE
Tel: 0171 589 3315
Fax: 0171 581 1357
email: mship@wexas.com
http://www.wexas.com/travel

© WEXAS International 1998
ISBN 0 905802 09 8

Cover design by Wylie Design Co., London
Printed and bound in UK by Clays Ltd. (Bungay, Suffolk)

CONTENTS

CHAPTER FOUR
Travellers' Diseases

CONTENTS

DIRECTORY

INTRODUCTION

In an age when travel to exotic and tropical places is practically run of the mill, and where adventure travel is top of the expenditure charts, the need for medical advice is increasingly necessary. Many illnesses and accidents abroad can be prevented with a basic knowledge of the possible hazards: *The Traveller's Healthbook* will answer the common questions asked by every type of traveller and allay many unwarranted fears.

The first chapter deals with the preparations to make before your departure. This is arguably the most nerve-racking part of the whole journey. What injections do you need to get? What supplies should you take in the medical bag? Do you need health insurance? What will the weather be like when you get there? Our expert contributors offer sensible down-to-earth advice to ensure that you will be in the know.

All aspects of air travel are tackled in Chapter Two. Perhaps you are a member of the "white-knuckle brigade" – the term air crews use for those with a fear of flying? Or maybe you suffer from jet lag? Whatever your complaints, you will get the low-down from specialists in the subject as to what to do.

In the third chapter, we get down to the nitty gritty of

problems on the road: aches, pains and sprains; healthy eating; the dilemma of accepting a blood transfusion in a developing country; overcoming culture shock and coming face to face with snakes and other nasties. We had no idea how many poisonous reptiles, insects and fish there were lurking out there for the unsuspecting traveller.

Wider issues are discussed in Chapter Four: malaria and the continuing controversy over which drugs to take; diarrhoeal illness; and the growing problem of HIV infection amongst the heterosexual travelling community. This chapter also includes a check-list of diseases – whether it be food poisoning or Japanese encephalitis – their symptoms and the cures available.

World health situations do change unexpectedly, so we have added a directory at the back of the book which lists travel clinics where you will be able to obtain the most specific and up-to-date information. The directory also has a country by country health profile, which will give you an idea as to the medical care available at your destination, and a vaccination requirement chart, to prepare you for the worst as you wait to have the necessary vaccinations.

However, it is worth remembering that it will be an unlucky traveller who meets with some of the more serious diseases out there, (take a look at the risk percentage chart on p. 203), and a quite exceptionally unlucky one who encounters them after having read about all the precautions that can be taken.

Bon santé en route.

Miranda Haines and Sarah Thorowgood

Chapter One
BEFORE YOU GO

PLANNING YOUR TRIP

by Drs Nick Beeching and Sharon Welby

The most carefully planned holiday, business trip or expedition may be ruined by illness, much of which is preventable. It is logical to put as much effort into protecting your health while abroad as you have into planning your itinerary and obtaining the necessary equipment and travel papers. Unfortunately, it is not in the best commercial interests of travel companies to emphasise the possible health hazards of destinations that are being sold to potential customers: most holiday brochures limit health warnings to the minimum legal requirements, and some travel agents are woefully ignorant of the dangers of travel to more exotic climates. We have recently treated a travel agent for life-threatening malaria caught on the Kenyan coast. He had not taken malaria prophylaxis, despite the long and widespread recognition of the dangers of malaria in this area.

Happily, travellers' health problems are usually more mundane. Fatigue from overwork before a business trip or much-needed holiday, the stress of travel itself, exposure to new climates and over-indulgence in rich food, alcohol and tobacco all contribute to increased vulnerability to illness. Short-lived episodes of diarrhoea affect up to 50 per cent of travellers, and up to one fifth of tourists on some Mediterranean package holidays will have mild respiratory prob-

13

lems such as head colds, 'flu-like illnesses or, rarely, more severe pneumonias such as legionnaires' disease. Sunburn or heat exhaustion are common, and accidents associated with unfamiliar sports such as skiing are an obvious hazard. The most common cause of death among expatriates is road traffic accidents – not exotic infections.

Pre-travel Health Check-list

Ideally, starting three months before you travel, consult your family doctor and specialist agencies as necessary to:

1. Obtain information about specific health problems at your destinations.

2. Consider current health, medical and dental fitness for travel and current medications.

3. Obtain adequate health insurance (and form E111 if travelling to an EC country).

4. Check again that health insurance is adequate.

5. Plan and obtain necessary immunisations and malaria prophylaxis (it is worth going to a vaccination clinic even if you have not left yourself enough time for a full course of injections).

6. Plan and obtain other medications and first aid items and any necessary documentation.

7. Consider need for first-aid training course.

If you decide to travel at short notice, it is still worth visiting you doctor or travel clinic before you go because malaria prevention can still be prescribed and vaccines given. Most vaccines will provide protection within a few days and some which take longer to become protective are still worth considering, especially if you are going on a longer trip. Perhaps you will feel a bit like a pin cushion, but the protection is worth the discomfort.

Information Sources

The depth of preparation required before travel clearly

depends on the general health of the individual and on his or her destination(s). In the last few years, accessible information on health for travellers has improved considerably and this chapter is intended as a starting point. Further information may be obtained from many of the organisations and publications listed in the directory at the back of this book.

Travellers to areas outside Europe, North America or Australasia are advised to invest in a copy of *Travellers' Health: How to Stay Healthy Abroad* (3rd edition OUP) by Dr Richard Dawood – a guide which contains a wealth of information on all aspects of travel medicine. This is updated by regular features in TRAVELLER magazine (published by WEXAS), and is particularly recommended for those planning to work abroad or embarking on prolonged overland trips or expeditions in remote areas.

British travellers should obtain the booklet *Health Advice for Travellers*, prepared by the Department of Health and the Central Office of Information (booklet T5). This contains details of the documentation required for entitlement to free medical care and can be obtained from Post Offices, GP surgeries and vaccination centres or by telephoning the Health Literature Line (Freephone 0800 555 777). The leaflet is also constantly updated on pages 460-464 of CEEFAX, and on the computerised data services PRESTEL and ISTEL, to which most travel agents have access. Other useful sources of information might be the websites of the Centres for Disease Control (**http://www.cdc.gov/**) and the World Health Organisation (**http://www.who.org/**).

When travelling outside Europe, it is wise to obtain information about compulsory immunisation requirements from the appropriate Embassy, Consulate or High Commission of each country that you plan to visit. However, do not expect their personnel to be able to give you general medical advice, and their information is not always as up to date as it should be.

British travellers to exotic locations should also consult their District Public Health Department, or one of the centres of specific expertise listed in our directory, for the latest information on immunisation requirements and malaria prophylaxis. Those planning to work abroad should try to contact an employee of the company to ensure that adequate provision for medical and dental care is provided within their contract. If necessary, they should also consider taking out health insurance in addition to company policies.

Medical and Dental Health

If in any doubt about possible hazards of travel because of a pre-existing medical condition, consult your family doctor. People with heart or chest problems, recurrent blood clots in the legs or lungs, recent strokes, uncontrolled blood pressure, epilepsy, psychiatric disorders or chronic sinus or ear problems may be at risk when flying.

Late pregnancy is a contra-indication to flying, diabetics taking medication will need special advice and the disabled will have specific requirements that may need to be conveyed to airline and airport authorities. People with chronic health problems or women who are obviously pregnant should ask their doctor to complete a standard airline form certifying their fitness for flying. This form should be obtained from the airline concerned.

Adequate supplies of all routinely-prescribed medications, including oral contraceptives, should also be obtained before departure. For short trips within Europe, these will be provided as NHS prescriptions. Those planning longer stays abroad should determine the availability of their medication overseas or take adequate supplies (you may need to pay for these on private prescription). It is also strongly recommended that you obtain a certificate from your doctor detailing the drugs prescribed, including the correct pharmacological name, as well as the trade name. This will be necessary to satisfy customs officials and you may need to obtain certified translations into appropriate languages. Some drugs readily obtainable in the UK are viewed with great suspicion elsewhere (codeine, for example, is considered a controlled drug in many countries, and tranquillisers such as diazepam can cause problems). Women working in Saudi Arabia should take adequate supplies of oral contraceptives and will need a certified Arabic translation of the certificate stating that the contraceptives have been prescribed for their personal use.

Those with recurring medical problems should also obtain a letter from their family doctor detailing the condition(s) – the letter can then be shown to doctors abroad if emergency treatment becomes necessary.

People with surgically implanted devices are also advised to carry a doctor's certificate to show security officials. Artificial hip replacements frequently set off metal detection security alarms at airports, as do indwelling intravenous central venous lines (e.g. Portacath). People with cardiac pacemakers are unlikely to run into problems due to electrical interference from British or North American airport metal detectors, but should try to avoid going through them and arrange instead for a personal body check by security officials.

Expatriates taking up a contract abroad will often have to submit to a detailed medical examination as a condition of employment. Many countries insist on a negative HIV-antibody test before allowing foreigners to work. Some will not allow any known HIV-positive individual to enter the country, despite advice from the World Health Organisation (WHO) that such regulations are ineffective as a means of controlling the spread of HIV infection.

HIV-positive travellers should consult their medical specialist and local support groups about specific travel insurance problems and the advisability of travel. Individuals with specific chronic health problems, such as epilepsy, diabetes or long term steroid treatment, should obtain a "Medic-alert" bracelet or similar, which is more easily located in a medical emergency than a card carried in a pocket.

Dental health is often taken for granted by British citizens who get a rude shock when faced with bills for dental work overseas. Those embarking on prolonged travel or work abroad, or planning to visit very cold areas, should have a full preventative dental check up before leaving.

Spare spectacles, contact lenses and contact lens solutions should also be obtained before travelling. If you are planning a vigorous holiday or expedition (e.g. skiing, hill-walking etc.) it might be a good idea to begin an appropriate fitness regime before departure.

On Your Return

On returning from a long trip, most travellers will experience some euphoria and elation, as well as family reunions and the interested enquiries of friends. After this, as relaxation, and possibly jet lag set in, a period of apathy, exhaustion and weariness can follow. Recognise this and allow a few quiet days if it is feasible. There are usually many pressures at this stage, especially if equipment is to be unpacked and sorted, photographs processed, etc.

Another pressure for most people is the none too welcome thought of returning to the mundane chores involved in earning one's daily bread. If your travels have been challenging, then a couple of recovery days will probably make you work more efficiently thereafter and cope more expeditiously with the thousands of tasks which seem to need your urgent attention.

After a time of excitement and adventure, some will go through a period of being restless and bored with the simple routine of home and work. They may not be aware of this temporary change in personality but their families certainly will be. Having pointed out this problem, we cannot suggest any way of overcoming it except perhaps to recommend that everyone concerned try to recognise it and be a little more tolerant than normal. This may not be a sensible time to make major decisions affecting career, family and business.

Some will be relieved to arrive in their hygienic homes after wandering in areas containing some of the world's more nasty diseases. Unfortunately, the risk of ill health is not altogether gone as you may still be incubating an illness acquired abroad – incubation periods for diseases such as hepatitis or malaria can be a few months, or, in the extreme case of rabies, a few years.

After your return, any medical symptoms or even just a feeling of debility or chronic ill health must not be ignored – medical help should be sought. Tell your physician where you have travelled, in detail, including brief stopovers. It may be that you are carrying some illness outside the spectrum normally considered. Sadly this has been known to cause mistaken diagnosis so that malaria, for example, has been labelled as influenza with occasionally fatal consequences.

Tropical worms and other parasites, enteric fevers, typhus, histoplasmosis (a fungal disease breathed in on guano, making cavers particularly vulnerable), tuberculosis, tropical virus diseases, amoebic dysentery and hepatitis may all need to be treated. For these illnesses to be successfully treated, many patients will need expert medical attention.

Routine tropical disease check-ups are provided by some companies for their employees during or after postings abroad. They are not generally necessary for other travellers who have not been ill whilst abroad, or after their return. People who feel that they might have acquired an exotic infection, or who have received treatment for infection abroad, should ask their doctor about referral to a unit with an interest in tropical diseases. Most health regions have a unit and more specialist centres are listed in the directory.

All unprotected sexual encounters while travelling carry high risks of infection with various sexually transmitted diseases in addition to HIV and hepatitis B. A post-travel check-up is strongly advised, even if you have no symptoms. Your local hospital will advise about the nearest clinic – variously called genito-urinary medicine (GUM) clinics, sexually-transmitted disease (STD) clinics, sexual health clinics, VD clinics or "special" clinics. Absolute anonymity is guaranteed, and no referral is needed from your GP.

After leaving malarial areas, many will feel less motivated to continue taking their antimalarial drugs. It is strongly recommended that these be taken for a minimum of 28 days after leaving the endemic area. Failure to do this has caused many travellers to develop malaria some weeks after they thought they were totally safe. This is more than a nuisance: it has occasionally proved fatal.

Fortunately, the majority of travellers return home with nothing other than pleasant memories of an enjoyable interlude in their lives.

GETTING KITTED OUT
by Drs Nick Beeching and Sharon Welby

Individual requirements vary greatly and most travellers do not need to carry enormous bags of medical supplies. This section covers a few health items that the majority of travellers should consider. Those going to malarious areas should read the advice given on malaria in Chapter Four, and those going to areas without ready access to medical care should read the article on health problems abroad, in Chapter Four, for further suggestions for their kit bag.

First-aid training is appropriate for travellers to remote

areas and those going on prolonged expeditions which might include a medical officer. As the medical needs of expeditions vary so much, an expedition kit bag list has not been included here. Expedition leaders should consult their own organisation or one of the specialist agencies for advice.

Painkillers: We always carry soluble aspirin (in foil-sealed packs) which is an excellent painkiller and reduces inflammation associated with sunburn (just be careful about the water you dissolve it in!). Aspirin should not be given to children aged less than twelve, and take paracetamol syrup for young children. Both paracetamol and aspirin reduce fever associated with infections.

Adults who cannot tolerate aspirin because of ulcer problems, gastritis or asthma should instead take paracetamol (not paracetamol/codeine preparations). To avoid potential embarrassment with customs officials, stronger painkillers should only be carried with evidence that they have been prescribed.

Cuts and grazes: A small supply of waterproof dressings (e.g. *Band-Aids*) is useful and a tube of antiseptic cream such as *Savlon* – especially if travelling with children.

Sunburn: British travellers frequently underestimate the dangers of sunburn and should take particular care that children do not get burnt. Protect exposed areas from the sun, remembering the back of the neck. Sunbathing exposure times should be gradually increased and use adequate sunblock creams (waterproof if swimming), particularly at high altitude where UV light exposure is higher. Sunburn should be treated with rest, plenty of non-alcoholic drinks and paracetamol or aspirin. Those who burn easily may wish to take a tube of hydrocortisone cream for excessively burnt areas. (See article *If You Can't Stand The Heat...* in Chapter Four.)

BEFORE YOU GO

Motion sickness: If liable to travel sickness, try to sleep through as much of the journey as possible and avoid reading. Also avoid watching the horizon through the window and, if travelling by boat, remain on deck as much as possible.

Several types of medication give potential relief from motion sickness when taken before the start of a journey, and sufferers should experiment to find out which suits them best. Antihistamines (e.g. *Phenergan*) are popular, especially for children, but should not be taken with alcohol. Adults should not drive until all sedative effects of antihistamines have worn off. Other remedies include *Kwells* (hyoscine tablets), *Dramamine* (dimenhydrinate) and *Stugeron* (cinnarazine). *Scopoderm* patches, only available on prescription, release hyoscine through the skin for up to three days. Hyoscine taken by mouth or by skin patch causes a dry mouth and can cause sedation.

Constipation: The immobility of prolonged travel, body clock disruption, dehydration during heat acclimatisation and reluctance to use toilets of dubious cleanliness all contribute to constipation. Drink plenty of fluids and try to eat a high fibre diet. Those who are already prone to constipation may wish to take additional laxatives or fibre substitutes (e.g. *Fybogel*).

Diarrhoea: Although this is a common problem, it is usually self-limiting and most travellers do not need to carry anti-diarrhoea medication with them (see the article *Diarrhoeal Illness* in Chapter Four). Diarrhoea reduces absorption of the contraceptive pill and women may wish to carry supplies of alternative contraceptives in case of this.

Female problems: Women who suffer from recurrent cystitis or vaginal thrush should consult their doctor to obtain appropriate antibiotics to take with them. Tampons are often difficult to buy in many countries and should be bought before travelling. Periods are often irregular or may cease altogether during travel but this does not mean that you cannot become pregnant.

Insect bites: Insect bites are a nuisance in most parts of the world and also transmit a variety of infections, the most important of which is malaria. Personal insect repellents will be needed by most travellers and usually contain DEET (diethyltoluamide). Liquid formulations are the cheapest but are less convenient to carry. Lotions and cream are available and sprays are the easiest to apply but are bulky to carry. Sticks of repellent are easier to carry and last the longest. All these should be applied to the skin and to clothing adjacent to exposed areas of skin, but should not be applied around the eyes, nose and mouth (take care with children).

DEET dissolves plastics, including carrier bags etc., so beware! An alternative to DEET-containing repellents is *Mosiguard Natural*. Marketed by MASTA, this is made from a blend of eucalyptus oils and is as effective as repellents based on DEET. It is more suitable for people who are sensitive to DEET.

When abroad, try to reduce the amount of skin available to biting insects by wearing long sleeves, and long trousers or skirts. If a mosquito net is provided with your bed, use it. Permethrin-impregnated mosquito nets are effective and can be purchased before travel to malarious areas. "Knockdown" insecticide sprays may be needed, and mosquito coils are easy to carry. Electric buzzers (that imitate male mosquito noises) are useless and candles and repellent strips (containing citronella) are not very effective. If bitten by insects, try to avoid scratching, which can introduce infection, particularly in the tropics. *Eurax* cream or calamine lotion can relieve local irritation, and antihistamine tablets may help those who have been bitten extensively.

Antihistamine creams should be used with caution as they can cause local reactions, and we prefer to use weak hydrocortisone cream on bites that are very irritating. Hydrocortisone cream should only be used if the skin is not obviously broken or infected. Increasing pain, redness, swelling or obvious pus suggest infection, and medical attention should be sought.

HIV prevention: Most HIV infections are acquired sexually (see article *HIV/AIDS and Sex Abroad* in Chapter Four). All adults should consider taking a supply of condoms. Travellers to countries with limited medical facilities should consider taking a supply of sterile needles and syringes so that injections required abroad are not given with re-usable needles of doubtful sterility.

Personal supplies of syringes and needles can make customs officials very suspicious, and condoms are not acceptable in some countries – particularly the Middle East.

To avoid problems at the border, it is worth buying these items as part of a small HIV/AIDS prevention pack which is available from most of the medical equipment suppliers listed in the directory. Larger "HIV prevention packs" which include blood product substitutes are rarely worth carrying.

VACCINES
by Drs. Nick Beeching and Sharon Welby

Immunisations may be necessary to prevent illnesses that are common in many countries but which are rarely encountered in Western Europe, North America or Australasia. In the UK you can get most vaccinations through a general practitioner or a specialised vaccination centre (see list in directory). Some will be free of charge, but the majority will have to be paid for privately. The exact requirements for a traveller will depend on his or her lifestyle, intended destinations and personal vaccination history, but should be considered at least two to three months before departure.

Modern immunisations are remarkably safe and well-tolerated. However, some vaccines contain traces of penicillin or neomycin and allergy to these antibiotics should be declared. Some vaccines are prepared in eggs and serious allergy to eggs will preclude some inoculations. Patients with chronic illness, particularly immune deficiency due to steroid treatment, cancer chemotherapy or HIV infection, should not receive most vaccines containing live organisms (such as oral polio vaccine), and pregnancy is also a contraindication for several vaccines.

International regulations cover the minimum legal requirements for a few vaccinations, particularly yellow fever and the meningitis A and C vaccine (required by pilgrims to Mecca, Saudi Arabia at the time of the Haj): cholera vaccine is no longer required or recommended (as stated by the 1973 World Health Assembly). However, in remote areas, border officials may occasionally ask to see certificates of people travelling from infected areas; such travellers are advised to carry a statement of the International Health Regulations documenting that "cholera is no longer a required entry condition" to any country, on official stationery, signed and stamped by a medical practitioner.

If in doubt about the need for International Certificates for yellow fever, it may be wise to obtain one before travel in order to avoid any possibility of being forced to accept a vaccination (using needles of dubious origin and sterility) on arrival at your destination.

It is equally important that the traveller has adequate protection against infections such as hepatitis A, polio and tetanus, even though proof of this will not be required by immigration officials at your destination. All travellers should have up-to-date tetanus immunisations, and travellers outside Europe, North America and Australasia should ensure that their polio immunisation is adequate. Children should have received all their childhood immunisations, but children who are going to live in the tropics should have early immunisation against tuberculosis (BCG) and hepatitis B infection as well.

The following list summarises information on the most commonly required vaccinations. For a guideline of requirements for each country see the *Country By Country Malaria Risk and Vaccination Guide* at the back of the directory. You can have as many vaccines as you like on one day, if you are feeling brave, but the live vaccines (poliomyelitis, yellow fever, BCG and MMR) should either be given on the same day or three weeks apart, otherwise the protection is reduced. The information below is in alphabetical order.

Cholera: A profuse diarrhoeal illness which poses little risk to the majority of travellers, and which is acquired from contaminated food or water. There have recently been large epidemics in much of South America and regions of Central Africa and the Indian subcontinent. Limited protection (about 50 per cent) is by vaccination, which ideally consists of two injections at least ten days apart. New oral vaccines recently licensed in Europe may become available in the future, and may be particularly useful for the high risk traveller.

Diphtheria: A booster dose of diphtheria vaccine is recommended for all travellers to the Russian Federation, Ukraine and Tajisktan and for longer-term visitors (more than four weeks) to Africa, Asia, and South America if the last vaccine dose was more than ten years ago. Routine immunisation started on a national scale in 1940, and travellers who are travelling to high risk places and have never been immunised should have a primary course of diphtheria (three doses of vaccine given one month apart).

Hepatitis A: A water-borne virus infection that poses a significant health hazard for travellers to all parts of the tropics. The illness has an incubation period of three to six weeks and causes lethargy and jaundice which may last for several weeks. The illness is often very mild in children aged less than five, and often goes completely unnoticed in this age group, so some adults will already have immunity even if they never had jaundice.

There are two options for protection. The old-fashioned immunisation with a gammaglobulin injection just prior to travel provides reasonable protection (a 2ml injection for two months and 4ml for four months), after which a repeat will be needed if still travelling. This is still a suitable option for the 'one off' traveller going on a short trip, but sometimes the gammaglobulin is not readily available. This option is less effective than vaccination.

Hepatitis A vaccine is safe and very effective. One dose of vaccine at least ten days before travelling gives good protection for at least one year. A booster dose six to twelve months later gives protection for ten years. The vaccine is expensive and certain people (with a past history of jaundice, or who have spent time in the tropics as a child, or who are over 50 years old) may benefit from having a blood test, because if it shows natural immunity a vaccination is not necessary.

Hepatitis B: A common infection in the tropics and countries bordering the Mediterranean, hepatitis B is caused by a virus that is transmitted by sex, by an infusion of contaminated blood or by sharing or reusing hypodermic needles. Hepatitis B shows similar symptoms to those of hepatitis A but sometimes is more severe and may lead to lasting liver damage. It is preventable with safe and highly effective injections given at three intervals, ideally with the second and third injections following at one and six month intervals after the first. An accelerated schedule can be given with a third dose at two months but a booster is needed at 12 months if the protection is to last for five years.

The vaccination is recommended for health workers and those working in refugee camps and similar environments, as well as for people planning to live in the tropics for more than six months. It should also be considered by all adults who might have sexual contact with travellers or with anyone living in areas where the infection is prevalent, and by all people who misuse intravenous drugs.

Combined hepatitis A and B vaccine: A new combined vaccine *Twinrix* is now available, which will give protection against both hepatitis A and hepatitis B. Three injections are required, the second is given one month later and the third at six months. Protection is given after the second injection and the booster dose will give further protection for five years. This vaccine is particularly useful for the frequent business traveller and the backpacker who has not been previously vaccinated, the advantage being the reduction in the number of vaccinations from five to three.

Japanese encephalitis: This is a rare virus infection causing severe encephalitis (inflammation of the brain) primarily in rural areas of Asia, especially during the rainy season. A moderately effective vaccine is obtainable only through specialist vaccination clinics and is usually restricted to those wandering off the beaten track for prolonged periods. Three injections spaced over one month provide protection at the end of the month which lasts for two years. The vaccine is associated with a low incidence of serious but treatable side-effects and is not recommended for people who have a history of "urticarial" rash ("hives").

Malaria: No vaccine available, see the article on malaria in Chapter Four for details about prevention.

Meningococcal meningitis: Epidemics recur in many parts

of sub-Saharan Africa (mainly in the dry season) and an epidemic which began in Nepal moved to many other countries via the 1987 Haj pilgrimage to Mecca. The Saudi Arabian authorities now require Haj pilgrims to provide certificates of vaccination against the infection, and a safe and effective vaccine against strains A and C of the organism is now available. This vaccine does not protect against strain B of the meningococcus which is the commonest strain found in the UK. The vaccine is not normally required by tourists unless travelling to an area with a current epidemic. Those working (especially in hospitals or schools) or travelling for more than four weeks in a region where the infection is common should have the vaccine. One injection at least ten days before travel provides protection for three years.

Poliomyelitis (polio):   Most adults have been immunised (immunisations started in 1958) but should receive a booster if this has not been given in the past ten years. Vaccination is usually given by mouth using a "live" polio virus variant that provides protection but does not cause illness. Patients with immune suppression can receive injections of killed organisms instead (the *Salk* vaccine).

Rabies: Vaccination for rabies before travel is safe but is usually reserved for those working with animals or those planning expeditions or employment in remote areas (see the article on rabies in Chapter Four for action to be taken if bitten). Three injections given subcutaneously over one month give protection for two years. The vaccine may also be given into the skin (intradermally); this smaller dose is an effective and cheaper alternative but is unlicensed. The intradermal route cannot be used if chloroquine is being taken concurrently for malaria prevention.

Smallpox: This vaccination is no longer required following the successful world-wide eradication of smallpox.

BEFORE YOU GO

Tetanus: Vaccination effectively prevents tetanus and a booster dose will be needed for adults who have not been immunised in the last ten years. Routine childhood immunisation did not begin in the UK until 1961 and older adults may need a full course of immunisation if they have missed out on this. However, if you have had a total of at least five tetanus vaccinations in your life, no further jabs are needed unless you have a tetanus-prone wound. We often advise travellers to have a tetanus booster before going to developing countries in order to avoid an injection in less ideal conditions, should they have a tetanus-prone injury. Any contaminated wounds received while abroad should be cleaned and medical consultation sought concerning the need for antibiotics and additional vaccination.

Tickborne encephalitis: There is an unlicensed vaccine available for this viral infection on a "named-patient only" basis. It is recommended for people going to walk, camp or work for prolonged periods in late spring and early summer in endemic areas. Two doses of vaccine given four to twelve weeks apart give protection for one year and a third dose at nine to twelve months extends protection for three years. The vaccine is usually well tolerated. If you have a tick bite in an endemic area remove the tick immediately and seek medical advice. A treatment is available (specific immunoglobulin) which is effective at preventing encephalitis if given within 72 hours of the tick bite.

Tuberculosis: Although this bacterial infection is widespread in the tropics, it does not pose a major hazard for most travellers. Most British (but not North American) adults, and children aged over thirteen, will have already been immunised against TB (BCG vaccination). Those embarking on prolonged travel or employment abroad should consult their doctor about their TB immune status. Pre-employment medical examinations usually include this.

Typhoid: This bacterial infection is acquired from contaminated food, water or milk in any area of poor sanitation outside Europe, North America or Australasia.

Typhoid vaccination is not necessary for most short-stay tourists, but should be considered by all visitors to the Indian subcontinent and those planning prolonged (more than four weeks) or remote travel in areas of poor hygiene. The old-fashioned TAB (typhoid and paratyphoid A and B vaccine) and typhoid vaccines are no longer used, as there are now several alternatives.

The older vaccine typhoid monovalent whole cell vaccine (two injections) provides moderate protection for about three years, after which a single booster dose is required. The vaccine commonly causes a sore arm and fever, especially in those who have had the vaccine before. The side-effects may be lessened if the vaccine is given in the skin tissues (intradermal injection). This vaccine is no longer available in the UK.

A new injected vaccine ("Typhim Vi") gives moderate protection after one dose and has less side effects. The vaccine gives three years' protection.

The third alternative is a course of capsules containing a live vaccine strain ("Ty 21a"), which is taken by mouth. It consists of three doses on alternate days. It may appeal to those with a phobia of needles, but the course is expensive, must be taken strictly according to the manufacturer's instructions and only provides immunity for one year, after which it will need to be repeated. It cannot be taken at the same time as oral polio vaccine or any antibiotic, or within twelve hours of taking mefloquine. As with other live vaccines, it is not recommended for pregnant women.

Yellow fever: This virus infection, causing a lethal hepatitis, is transmitted by mosquitoes and is restricted to parts of Africa and South and Central America. It can be prevented by a highly effective and safe vaccine, which has to be administered in a designated centre and recorded on a specific internationally-recognised certificate. The certificate is valid for ten years, starting ten days after vaccination.

MEDICAL INSURANCE
by Ian Irvine

No matter how carefully you read this book, sickness and accidents may nevertheless occur whilst you are travelling, and the wise traveller needs to be aware of the best action to take to ensure that when the chips are down, he has the best possible care.

The most important step to attaining this is being aware that *no one should travel without medical insurance*. It is essential to make sure that the medical insurance is adequate (currently not less than one million pounds), includes repatriation cover to the insured person's country of residence, does not have unusual exclusions, covers all activities in which the traveller is likely to participate and has an emergency service available at all times to provide assistance. If you have any doubt at all about insurance you should consult a registered insurance broker, who will be happy to assist you without cost.

If you are suffering from any medical condition, you must disclose full particulars to your medical insurers before arranging the insurance. Whilst you have a duty to do this, it does also give your insurers an opportunity to assess your condition and possibly offer advice. They will also notify you of any limitations which might apply to the medical insurance because of such a condition.

In general terms, medical claims for sickness and accident fall into two separate categories. There are those which are not serious, normally of short duration and the costs for which are comparatively minor. Most sensible travellers, with appropriate medical advice, can sort out such incidents without difficulty and whilst incurring expenditure, can normally pay for this themselves and recover their outlay under medical insurance on their return to the UK. More serious medical problems can cause difficulty, are normally of long duration and sometimes necessitate the cancellation of travel and the return home of the traveller. It is impossible to issue guidelines for every type of travel situation, but suffice it to say that medical opinion of any sickness or accident should be sought. Immediate action should also be taken to prevent any deterioration in health and urgent arrangements made for the appropriate medical treatment to be given.

In the event of a serious accident or illness, the emergency service provided by medical insurers should be contacted at the earliest opportunity and full details of the sickness or accident given. Very often treatment overseas is only available when it is known that payment is guaranteed and most travellers are not in a position to do this. This facility is provided by the emergency service of the medical insurers, and once they have full details of the problem and have had an opportunity to discuss the course of action to be taken with local medical advisers, they are normally quite prepared to guarantee the cost of the treatment. This may relate to hospital charges, doctors', surgeons' or anaesthetists' fees, medication and transportation, all of which is quite normal and something the emergency service is used to handling. Sometimes a traveller may suffer from an illness or accident in a remote location where there are inadequate medical facilities. In this situation, movement to a location which has better facilities may be necessary and this is something which the emergency service will organise and coordinate within the terms of the policy.

In the event of a very serious problem, it is sometimes impossible to arrange for treatment to UK standards to be provided locally and, if such a situation should arise, repatriation to the UK may become necessary. Equally, if a traveller has suffered a serious illness or accident, has received some treatment and is making a recovery but is unwell enough to return to the UK without assistance, then repatriation may also be provided. The emergency services of the medical insurers are experienced in arranging repatriation and whether this necessitates a row of seats on an aircraft, or a special medical jet with a medical team on board will be determined by the emergency service and then appropriate arrangements will be made and coordinated by them to ensure the traveller's safe return home.

Reciprocal health agreements exist in certain foreign countries, although these normally only relate to direct costs incurred for medical treatment. They certainly do not provide for any repatriation or transportation costs and therefore do not mean that medical insurance should not be acquired.

The principal area of reciprocal health agreements is within the European Community, and to secure treatment the traveller must carry an E111 form, which can be obtained from any Department of Social Security office. This is a certificate which entitles the bearer to health benefits during a stay in a member country of the European Community. The regulations for each country in the European Community do differ, as does the level of benefit available, and details are currently available in the Department of Social Security leaflet N138.

British residents travelling to Australia are entitled to reciprocal health arrangements under the Medicare scheme and whilst medical facilities in Australia are superb, no repatriation or transportation cover is provided, which, if necessary, could result in a heavy expenditure. For that reason it is particularly important that travellers to Australia should arrange medical insurance.

Elsewhere in the world, including North America, it is most unlikely that any medical treatment will be available without either being paid for at the time, or guaranteed by the emergency service of medical insurers, and such being the case, it is a fool who travels without proper cover.

WEXAS Annual Traveller Insurance

Members of WEXAS can take advantage of a choice of two annual policies for multiple journeys.

1. The Holiday Traveller annual policy costs £60 a year for Europe and £69 a year world-wide. This policy provides cover for up to a maximum of 31 days' travel per trip and includes winter sports cover for up to 17 days a year.

2. The Global Traveller annual policy costs £99 a year and provides cover for both business and leisure travel up to a maximum of 92 days per trip. Winter sports cover for up to 21 days a year is also included.

All WEXAS Traveller insurance policies provide an extensive medical cover of up to £5,000,000.

Conclusion

How often have we heard the old adage "prevention is better than cure"? For travellers this is particularly relevant and the further afield you travel, and the more remote the location, the more relevant these words become. Notwithstanding this, it is inevitable that sickness and accidents do occur from time to time, and, if they are serious, even the most experienced traveller will need assistance.

A GUIDE TO SEASONAL TRAVEL
by Paul Pratt and Melissa Shales

Africa

North: The climate here varies widely from the warm and pleasant greenery of a Mediterranean climate in the coastal regions to the arid heat of the deep Sahara. Rains on the coast usually fall between September and May and are heavy but not prolonged. It can get cool enough for snow to settle in the mountainous areas, but temperatures will not usually fall below freezing, even in winter. In summer, temperatures are high (up to around 40°C) but bearable.

The Sahara, on the other hand, is extreme, with maximum summer temperatures of around 50°C and minimum winter temperatures of around 3°C. The temperature can fall extremely rapidly, with freezing nights following blisteringly hot days. What little, if any, rain there is can fall at any time of the year. The desert is also prone to strong winds and dust storms.

West: At no time is the climate in West Africa likely to be comfortable, although some areas and times of the year are worse than others. The coastal areas are extremely wet and humid, with up to 2500mm of rain falling in two rainy seasons (May and June and then again in October). In the north there is considerably less rain, with only one wet period between June and September. However, the humidity is still high, only lessened by the arrival of the *harmattan*, a hot, dry and dusty north-easterly wind which blows from the Sahara. Temperatures remain high and relatively even throughout the year.

East: Although much of this area is on or near the equator, little of it has an "equatorial" climate. The lowlands of Djibouti in the extreme east have a very low, uncertain rainfall, creating near-desert conditions plagued by severe droughts. Further down the coast, the high lowland temperatures are moderated by constant sea breezes. The temperatures inland are brought down by high altitude plateaux and mountain ranges to about the level found in Britain at the height of summer. Temperatures are reasonably stable all year round although the Kenya highlands have a cooler, cloudy "winter" from June to September. There are rainy seasons in most areas in April and May and for a couple of months between July and November, depending on the latitude.

South: The whole area from Angola, Zambia and Malawi southwards tends to be fairly pleasant and healthy, although there are major variations from the Mediterranean climate of Cape Province with its mild winters and warm, sunny summers, to the semi-desert sprawl of the Kalahari and the relatively wet areas of Swaziland, inland Mozambique and the Zimbabwe highlands to the east. In the more northern areas, there is a definite summer rainy season from December to March when the temperatures are highest. On the south coast, there is usually some rain all year round. The west coast, with little rain, has cloud and fog due to the cold Benguela current which also helps keep down the temperature. The best times of the year to visit are April, May and September when the weather is fine but not too hot or humid.

North America

Almost half of Canada and most of the north of Alaska is beyond the Arctic Circle and suffers from the desperately harsh weather associated with this latitude. The ground is tundra and rarely melts for more than a couple of feet and even though summer temperatures are often surprisingly high, the summers are short-lived. Snow and frost are possible at any time of the year, while the northern areas have permanent snow cover. The coast is ice bound for most of the year.

The whole centre of the continent is prone to severe and very changeable weather, as the low-lying land of the Great Plains and the Canadian Prairies offers no resistance to sweeping winds that tear across the continent both from the Gulf and the Arctic. The east is fairly wet but the west has very little rain, resulting in desert and semi-desert country in the south.

Winter temperatures in the north can go as low as -40°C and can be very low even in the south, with strong winds and blizzards. In the north, winter is long-lived. Summers are sunny and often scorchingly hot.

In general, the coastal areas of North America are far kinder than the centre of the continent. The Pacific coast is blocked by the Rockies from the sweeping winds, and in the Vancouver area the climate is similar to that of the UK. Sea breezes keep it cool further south.

Seasons change fairly gradually on the east coast, but the northerly areas still suffer from the extremes of temperature which give New York its fabled humid heatwaves and winter temperatures. New York, in spite of being far further north, is often much hotter than San Francisco. The Newfoundland area has heavy fog and icebergs for shipping to contend with. Florida and the Gulf States to the south have a tropical climate, with warm weather all year round, and winter sun and summer thunderstorms. This is the area most likely to be affected by hurricanes and tornadoes, although cyclones are possible throughout the country.

Mexico and Central America

The best time to visit this area is during the dry season (winter) from November to April. However, the mountains and the plains facing the Caribbean have heavy rainfall throughout the year, which is usually worst from September to February. The mountains and plains facing the Pacific have negligible rainfall from December to April.

Central and northern Mexico tend to have a longer dry season and the wet season is seldom troublesome to the traveller as it usually rains only between 4pm and 5pm. The temperature is affected by the altitude. The unpleasant combination of excessive heat and humidity at the height of the wet season should be avoided at the lower altitudes.

South America

The climatic conditions of the South American continent are determined to a great extent by the trade winds which, if they originate in high pressure areas, are not necessarily carriers of moisture. With a few regional exceptions, rain in South America is confined to the summer months, both north and south of the Equator. The exceptions are: (i) South Brazil and the eastern coast of Argentina and Uruguay; (ii) the southern Chilean coastal winter rainfall region; (iii) the coastal area of northeast Brazil.

The highest rainfall in South America is recorded in the Amazon basin, the coast lands of Guyana and Suriname and the coastlines of Colombia, Ecuador and southwest Chile. Altitude determines temperature, especially in the Andean countries near to the equator: hot – up to 1000 metres; temperate – 1000 to 2000 metres; cold – above 2000 metres.

Argentina: The winter months, June to October, are the best time for visiting Argentina. Buenos Aires can be oppressively hot and humid from mid-December to the end of February. Climate ranges from the sub-tropical north to sub-antarctic in Tierra del Fuego.

Brazil: The dry season runs from May to October apart from the Amazon Basin and the Recife area which have a tropical rainy season from April to July.

Bolivia: Heavy rainfall on the high western plateau from May to November. Rains in all seasons to the eastern part of the country.

Chile: Just over the border from Bolivia, one of the driest deserts in the world faces the Pacific coast.

Ecuador: Dry seasons from June to October. The coast is very hot and wet, especially during the period December to May. The mountain roads can be very dangerous during the wet season owing to landslides.

Paraguay: The best time for a visit is from May to October when it is relatively dry. The heaviest rainfall is from December to March, at which time it is most likely to be oppressively hot and humid.

Peru: During the colder months, June to November, little rainfall but damp on the coast, high humidity and fog. From December to May, travel through the mountains can be hazardous owing to heavy rain which may result in landslides, causing road blockage and long delays.

Paraguay: The best time for a visit is from May to October when it is relatively dry. The heaviest rainfall is from December to March, at which time it is most likely to be oppressively hot and humid.

The Far East and Southeast Asia

Hong Kong: Subtropical climate; hot, humid and wet summer with a cool, but generally dry winter. Typhoon season is usually from July to August. The autumn, which lasts from late September to early December, is the best time for visiting as the temperature and humidity will have fallen and there are many clear, sunny days. Macao has a similar climate but the summers are a little more bearable on account of the greater exposure to sea breezes. There is also an abundance of trees for shelter during the hot summer.

Japan: Japan lies in the northern temperate zone. Spring and autumn are the best times for a visit. With the exception of Hokkaido, the large cities are extremely hot in summer. Hokkaido is very cold in winter. Seasonal vacation periods, especially school holidays, should be avoided if one is going to enjoy visiting temples, palaces and the like in relative comfort.

Korea: Located in the northern temperate zone, with spring and autumn the best times for touring. The deep blue skies of late September/October and early November, along with the warm sunny days and cool evenings, are among Korea's most beautiful natural assets. Though it tends to be rather windy, spring is also a very pleasant time for a Korean visit. There is a short but pronounced wet season starting towards the end of June and lasting into early August. Over 50 per cent of the year's rain falls during this period and it is usually very hot and humid.

Malaysia: There are no marked wet or dry seasons in Malaysia. October to January is the wettest period on the east coast, October/November on the west coast. Sabah has an equable tropical climate; October and April/May are usually the best times for a visit. Sarawak is seldom uncomfortably hot but is apt to be extremely wet. Typhoons are almost unknown in East Malaysia.

Thailand: Hot, tropical climate with high humidity. Best time for touring is from November to February. March to May is extremely hot and the wet season arrives with the southwest monsoon during June and lasts until October.

Singapore: Like Malaysia, Singapore has no pronounced wet or dry season. The even, constant heat is mitigated by sea breezes. The frequent rain showers have a negligible cooling effect.

BEFORE YOU GO

The Philippines: The Philippines have a similar climate to Thailand. The best time to travel in the islands is during the dry season, November to March. March to May is usually dry and extremely hot. The southwest monsoon brings the rain from May to November. The islands north of Samar through Luzon are prone to be affected by typhoons during the period July to September. The Visayas Islands, Mindanao and Palawan, are affected to a lesser degree by the southwest monsoon and it is still possible to travel comfortably during the wet season south of Samar Island – long sunny periods are usually interspersed with heavy rain.

Indian Subcontinent

Sri Lanka: The southwest monsoon brings rain from May to August in Colombo and in the southwest generally, while the northeast monsoon determines the rainy season from November to February in the northeast. The most popular time for a visit is during the northern hemisphere's winter.

India: The climate of south India is similar to that of Southeast Asia: warm and humid. The southwest monsoon brings the rainy season to most parts of India, starting in the southwest and spreading north and east from mid-May through June. Assam has an extremely heavy rainfall during monsoon seasons. Generally speaking, the period from November to April is the best time to visit. From April until the start of the southwest monsoon, the northern Indian plains are extremely hot, though the northern hill stations provide a pleasant alternative until the start of the monsoon rains. These places usually have a severe winter.

Nepal: March is pleasant, when all the rhododendrons are in bloom. The monsoon rains begin in April.

Middle East

A large proportion of this area is desert – flat, low-lying land with virtually no rain and some of the hottest temperatures on earth. Humidity is high along the coast and travellers should beware of heat exhaustion and even heat stroke. What little rain there is falls between November and March. To the north, in Iran and Iraq, the desert gives way to the great steppes, prone to extremes of heat and cold, with rain in winter and spring.

Melting snow from the surrounding mountains causes spectacular floods from March to May. The climate is considerably more pleasant in the Mediterranean areas with long, hot, sunny summers and mild, wet winters. The coast is humid, but even this is tempered by steady sea breezes. The only really unpleasant aspect of the climate here is the hot, dry and dusty desert wind which blows at the beginning and end of summer.

Europe

Only in the far north and those areas a long way from the sea does the climate in Europe get to be extreme. In northern Scandinavia and some of the inland eastern countries such as Bulgaria, there are long, bitterly cold winters with heavy snow and, at times, arctic temperatures. In western Europe, the snow tends to settle only for a few days at a time. In Britain, the Benelux countries and Germany, winter is characterised chiefly by continuous cloud cover, with rain or sleet. In the Alps, heavy snow showers tend to alternate with brilliant sunshine, offering ideal conditions for winter sports. There are four distinct seasons, and while good weather cannot be guaranteed during any of them, all are worth seeing. Summer is generally short, and the temperature varies widely from one year to the next, climbing at times to match that on the Mediterranean. For sun worshippers, the Mediterranean is probably the ideal location, hot for much of the year but rarely too hot or humid to be unbearable. Rain falls in short, sharp bursts, unlike the con-

tinuous drizzle to be found further north. Winter is mild and
snow rare.

Australasia

Australia: For such a vast land mass, there are few variations in the weather here. A crescent-shaped rain belt fol-
lows the coast to provide a habitable stretch around the
enormous semi-desert "outback". The Snowy Mountains in
the east do, as their name suggests, have significant snow-
falls, although even here it does not lie long. The east is the
wettest part of the country owing to trade winds which blow
off the Pacific. The rainfall pattern varies throughout the
country: the north and northeast have definite summer rains
between November and April; the south and west have winter rains; while in the east and southeast the rains fall year-
round. Tropical cyclones with high winds and torrential rain
occur fairly frequently in the northeast and northwest. Tasmania, further south and more mountainous, has a temperate climate similar to Britain's.

New Zealand: Although at a different latitude, the great
expanse of water around New Zealand gives it a maritime
climate similar to Britain's. The far north has a sub-tropical
climate with mild winters and warm, humid summers. There
are year-round snow fields in the south, and snow falls on
most areas in winter. Although the weather is changeable,
there is a surprising amount of sunshine, making this country ideal for most outdoor activities. The best time to visit is
from December to March, at the height of summer.

Papua New Guinea: The climate here is a fairly standard
tropical one – hot and wet all year, although the time and
amount of the rains are greatly influenced by the high mountains that run the length of the country. The rains are heavy,
but not continuous. While the coast tends to be humid, the
highlands are pleasant.

THE ALTERNATIVE WAY: Homeopathic Remedies

by Miranda Haines

Each time I go abroad to Nepal, Vietnam, India, even Thailand or Colombia, I get sick. Diarrhoea, heat stroke and general malaise strike ruthlessly despite the care I take over water, food, sleep and sun. On one occasion I ended up in an Indian hospital, on an intravenous drip for three days, due to a mysterious virus that never did find a name. Luckily the Indian doctor was superb, to whom I am eternally grateful, and we became good friends.

However, on my last trip to Morocco, not wanting to go to such extremes to find a new friend, I decided to take a different approach to my health abroad. Instead of begging my GP to prescribe anti-biotics for the illnesses that seemed inevitable, spending a small-fortune in the chemist on every possible drug available and then being unduly paranoid about foreign bodies on arrival, I paid a visit to my local herb shop.

Prevention, I decided, was going to be better than depending on a cure. Here, the herbal nutritionist recommended that I take capsules of *echinacea* to boost my immune and lymphatic systems. This, he assured me, would be good for preventing colic, colds, flu and other infections that I might catch on the aeroplane, or thereafter: and *acidophilus*, which is a type of "friendly" bacteria that one finds in live yoghurt. This would assist in the digestion of proteins, help reduce cholesterol levels, and enhance the absorption of nutrients, which all sounded good to me. But would it work?

Willing to give anything a try, I took the capsules three times a day for three weeks. All I can say in the herbs' defence, is that my three travel companions got mildly sick at various times of our trip and I felt not a twinge of anything wayward, despite eating *tagines* for England.

In a bid to explain why this may have worked for me, I went to Neil's Yard in Convent Garden and met with John Renshaw, a Chinese herbalist, who has been practising for seven years. He has seen a steady increase in the amount of travellers coming to his shop, *East West Herbs*, for alternative remedies. Renshaw spoke in philosophical soundbites to explain a Chinese herbalists' approach to medicine: "If a traveller coughs at an Indian in a virgin Amazon rainforest then the Indian might die – another traveller would just get a cold." In other words, unfamiliar germs have a dramatically different effect on those people already exposed to the pathogens, than those who have never encountered them before (i.e. the traveller).

Travellers are increasingly interested in alternative medicine, although no studies have been done as to why, and to what effect. However, two reasons seem likely: many people are developing a resistance to antibiotics; and other medicines like *Flagyl* – taken for amoebic dysentery and which can be harmful to the liver – can have damaging side-effects. So, if there is an alternative, then some people are seeking them out. Also, experienced long-haul travellers know that many medicines are simply not available readily in many countries, or, if they are, the doses are can be unreliable.

Sarah Chamberlaine, a website editor for Oxfam, is a frequent traveller and has always used natural remedies to keep her on the road. A week before leaving Chamberlaine takes garlic pills in order to make her stomach inhospitable to parasites. "I was once in California and I had a temperature of 104ºC. *Advil* and all the normal pills that you take just wouldn't bring my fever down. So, I contacted Joanne Alexander, of *Snowmountain Botanicals*, and she advised me to take a Chinese pill called *Ying Chow* which broke my fever within an hour."

Joanne Alexander has studied the art of homeopathic and herbal medicine, in China and Taiwan, and produces her own organically homegrown tinctures which she sells all over the world via her website. Alexander is available for consultation via email (smb@pacific.net) and will make up personal recipes and remedies for anyone who wishes. In fact, a search on the World Wide Web turns up a vast array of clubs and herbal practitioners.

Whether this 2000-year-old art is truly effective has not been proven by the medical authorities – although the royal establishment, Prince Charles and Princess Anne, both advocate the use of herbal remedies. What is certain is that everything must be prescribed by a trained herbalist or homeopath. This is important because doses of anything administered wrongly can be extremely harmful. If you are in doubt, there are several organisations to check with according to your needs. *Please note that this advice is not intended as a substitute for visiting your GP or travel clinic before leaving, and any serious injuries and illnesses should never be treated without seeking expert advice.*

Homeopathic remedies for the traveller are listed in a comprehensive leaflet produced by *Helios Homeopathic Pharmacy* (listed on p. 204 of the directory) that comes with a travel kit consisting of 36 herbs for £36.95. Even anti-malarial and vaccination remedies are sold in homeopathic pharmacies. The range of herbs, tinctures, essential oils and flower bach remedies are extensive and can be tried for most traveller ailments: jet lag, malaria, fear of flying, shock, dysentery, diphtheria – to name a few.

Here are a few examples: for jet lag there is a product called *Time Zone*, which is a herbal alternative to melatonin, and also recommend is arnica, which is good for exhaustion, ankle-swelling and insomnia; ginseng is thought to help the body relax and vitamins, C, E, B1 and B6 help rejuvenate the metabolism; pure oxygen, O-PUR (£9.99) combats bad air-conditioning on the aeroplane and is particularly recommended for asthmatics; ginseng is also thought to help motion sickness; for sunburn, aloe vera is recommended in combination with a strong sunscreen and head covering; in order to keep a tan longer beta carotene can be taken a week prior to departure; to keep the skin supple zinc and vitamin A supplements can be taken; urtica urens is a soothing ointment for hot, itchy skin that has minor burns, sunburn or allergic reactions to insect bites and stings; pyrethrum spray is a homeopathic insect repellent and bite soother and calendula is the alternative antiseptic ointment to use on cuts, broken or sore skin.

Neil's Yard Remedies also sell a Travel Roll for £32.50 that contains: lavender essential oil (relaxing oil that can be applied to relieve insect bites as it has antiseptic properties); hypericum & calendula tincture (antiseptic lotion); arnica ointment (use after bruising or injury); arnica tablets (help to reduce bruising and ameliorate shock); citronella essential oil (helps to repel mosquitoes and other insects); hypericum & urtica ointment; five flower remedy (for all first aid situations); camomile tea bags (can aid digestion). They also sell a *Basic Homeopathy Kit* for £24.95 which has a self-help information sheet.

Yet, with all this knowledge of herbs, I would never leave home without aspirin, savlon and water purification tablets. If homesickness should strike then the Honeysuckle Bach Flower remedy claims to work wonders. Naturally! Although, personally, I would buy an open-ended ticket, just in case.

For a list of useful addresses and further reading see p. 204 of the directory.

Chapter Two
AIR TRAVEL

FEAR OF FLYING

by Sheila Critchley

More people fly today than ever before, yet many experienced air travellers, as well as novices, suffer anguish and apprehension at the mere thought of flying. A survey by Boeing suggested that as many as one out of seven people experience anxiety when flying and that women outnumber men two to one in these feelings of uneasiness. The crews know them as "the white-knuckle brigade".

A certain amount of concern is perhaps inevitable. The sheer size of modern jet aircraft, which appear awkward and unwieldy on the ground, makes one wonder how they will manage to get into the air – and stay there. Most of these fears are irrational and are perhaps based on the certain knowledge that as passengers, once we are in the aircraft we are powerless to control our fate (this being entirely dependent on the skill and training of the crew). These nervous travellers find little comfort in the numerous statistical compilations which show that modern air transport is many times safer than transport by car or rail.

According to Lloyds of London it is 25 times safer to travel by air than by car. A spokesman for Lloyd's Aviation Underwriting said that if you consider all the world's airlines, there are some 600 to 1000 people killed every year

51

on average. This figure compares to an annual toll on the roads of some 55,000 in the United States, 12,000 in France and 5000 in the UK. One sardonic pilot used to announce on landing,"You've now completed the safest part of your journey. Drive carefully".

Anxiety

Most people's fear remains just that – anxiety which gives rise to signs of stress but remains on a manageable scale. For others, however, the anxiety can become an unimaginable fear, known as aviophobia or fear of flying. Symptoms include feelings of panic, sweating, palpitations, depression, sleeplessness, weeping spells, and sometimes temporary paralysis. Phobias are deep-seated and often require therapy to search out the root cause. Psychologists studying aviophobia suggest that in serious cases, there may be an overlap with claustrophobia (fear of confined places) and aerophobia (fear of heights).

Professional help can be obtained from specialists in behavioural psychotherapy. However, unlike other phobias which may impair a person's ability to function in society, those suffering from aviophobia may simply adopt avoidance of air travel as a means of coping. Only those whose lifestyles necessitate a great deal of foreign travel are forced into finding a solution.

One source of many people's fear of flying is simply a lack of knowledge about how an aircraft works and about which sounds are usual and to be expected. Visiting airports and observing planes taking off and landing can help overcome this problem. Reading about flying can also help (though air disaster fiction can hardly be recommended).

What To Do...

Talking to other people who fly regularly can also be reassuring. Frequent air travellers are familiar with the sequence of sounds that indicate that everything is proceeding normally: the dull "thonk" when the landing gear retracts on take-off; and the seeming deceleration of the engines at certain speeds, among other things. Since most people are familiar with the sounds in their cars and listen almost subconsciously to the changed "tones" that indicate mechanical difficulties, those aircraft passengers who are unsure about flying often feel a certain disquiet when they cannot distinguish "normal" from "abnormal" sounds in an aircraft.

Air turbulence can also be upsetting. Most modern aircraft fly above areas of severe winds (such as during thunderstorms) and pilots receive constant reports of upcoming weather conditions. Nonetheless, air currents up to 20,000 feet may buffet aircraft and the "cobblestoning" effect can be frightening even to experienced air travellers. Flight crews are aware of this problem and usually make an announcement to allay undue worries.

If you are afraid to fly, tell the stewardess when you board so that the crew can keep an eye on you. Hyperventilation is a common symptom of anxiety; the cure is to breathe slowly and deeply into a paper bag. Remember that all aircraft crew are professionals; their training is far more rigorous than, say, that required to obtain a driving licence.

Emergencies

It is probably worth mentioning that the cabin crew's main responsibility is not dispensing food and drink to passengers but rather the safety of everyone on board. There is usually a minimum of one flight attendant for every 50 passengers. The briefings on emergency procedures which are given at the beginning of every flight are not routine matters: they can mean the difference between life and death and should be taken seriously. Each type of aeroplane has different positions for emergency exits and for oxygen supplies, and different designs and positioning of life jackets. The air crew's demonstration of emergency procedures are for the benefit of everyone on board and should be watched and listened to attentively. In an emergency situation, reaction is vital within the first 15 seconds – there is no time to discover that you do not know where the emergency exits are situated. Learning about what to do in an emergency should reduce fear, not increase it.

Relaxation

One way of coping with fear of flying (at least in the short term) is to learn how to relax. In fact, in-flight alcohol (in sensible quantities), movies, reading material and taped music are all conducive to relaxation.

If these are not sufficient to distract you, some airlines conduct programmes for those they call "fearful flyers". These seminars consist of recorded tapes offering advice on relaxation techniques, statistical information on how safe it really is, group discussions where everyone is encouraged to discuss their fears and recorded simulations of the sounds to be expected in flight.

Familiarisation is the key concept behind all of these behaviourist therapy programmes; instruction in rhythmic deep breathing and sometimes even hypnosis can assist the person in learning to control his or her physical signs of anxiety. A graduate of one of these programmes confirmed its beneficial effects: "I enjoyed the course, especially sharing my misgivings with other people and discovering I wasn't alone with my fears. At the end of the course, we actually went up on a one-hour flight and I was able to apply all the techniques I had learned. In fact, I actually managed to enjoy the flight – something I would not have ever believed I could do".

A certain amount of anxiety about flying is to be expected. For most people, a long distance flight is not something one does every day. On the other hand, there is always a first time for everyone – even those who have chosen to make flying their career. The more you fly, the more likely you are to come to terms with your fears. Some anxiety is inevitable, but in the case of flying, the statistics are on your side.

Recommended Reading: *Taking the Fear Out of Flying* (David and Charles)

JET LAG
by Jack Barker

Jet lag affects every air traveller to some degree. A major survey by FARSA, New Zealand's flight crew union, found in 1994 that 96 per cent of flight attendants arriving in New Zealand, one of the world's longest haul destinations, complained of jet lag symptoms that included tiredness, loss of energy, broken sleep and impaired motivation. Even those who claim they are immune often give themselves away by revealing slips of bad temper, and often deny the symptoms in an attempt to override their body's natural reaction to international air travel.

The symptoms of jet lag include disorientation and confusion, as well as irritability and irrational anger. The most obvious symptom is tiredness, with many travellers feeling drained for days, as well as finding that they lack concentration and motivation. This can affect business skills as well as impair the enjoyment of a holiday. Unfortunately, another symptom is that travellers wake in the middle of the night and want to fall asleep during the day, which makes recovery from tiredness more difficult. These symptoms can last for some time: NASA estimates you need one day for every time-zone crossed to recover normal rhythm and energy patterns.

The situation is further complicated by some very obvious factors that ensure that air travel is a physically stressful experience. Dehydration caused by the aircraft's compression can cause headaches, dry skin, and nasal irritation, which make travellers more susceptible to the common and exotic viruses and bacteria given off by their fellow passengers and recirculated by the confined airflow system. The World Health Organisation links jet lag with the high incidence of digestive disorders abroad. Estimating that about 50 per cent of long distance travellers suffer from digestive problems, their report suggests that, "travel fatigue and jet lag may aggravate the problem by reducing travellers' resistance and making them more susceptible". The decompression and forced inactivity can also cause the swelling of limbs and feet which sometimes prevents travellers wearing their normal shoes for up to 24 hours on arrival. This is dangerous because swollen legs can cause blood clots which, when they break free, can lodge in the lungs and cause a pulmonary embolism. A 1988 report in the Lancet estimated that over three years at Heathrow Airport, 18 per cent of the 61 sudden deaths in long distance passengers were caused by clots on the lungs, a figure far higher than the incidence in the general population.

The main cause of jet lag is crossing time zones. This has the effect of putting the body's "Circadian Rhythms", which dictate what time you go to sleep, wake up and have meals, out of phase with the timescale of your new destination. Circadian Rhythms are maintained by minute releases of hormones and seratonins in the blood to dictate appetite and sleep patterns. As these chemical triggers were developed when we were living in caves, it is perhaps understandable that they have trouble adapting to travel by supersonic plane and it takes them some time to settle down to a new routine in a different time zone. Travellers flying East generally report worse symptoms, but lesser symptoms are also displayed going West and even those flying North or South or vice versa are not immune. Many travellers feel that day flights incur less severe jet lag but this might be partly because they miss less sleep while travelling.

There are a number of simple steps that travellers can take to minimise the worst effects of jet lag.

1. As soon as you are settled on the plane, adjust your watch to match the new time zone and start to try to think on the daily schedule of your destination.

2. Sleep. By far the best way to get through the minor stresses and discomforts of a long flight is to get plenty of rest. Blindfold masks, neckrests, and earplugs can all help. Kick off your shoes — although if your feet are likely to swell, make sure your shoes are a type you will be able to fit back on at the end of the flight. Although sleeping is good, resist the temptation to take sleeping pills to make certain of rest. This causes near-comatose immobility, little or no movement increases the chance of blood clots.

3. Drink water. Coffee dehydrates and tea also contains tannin, especially when poured from a cool airline teapot. Orange squash is also an abrasive drink, especially for people not accustomed to it. Alcohol has an increased effect in the rarified atmosphere of a pressurised plane and aggravates both dehydration and the swelling of limbs and feet. A good hangover might mask the effects of jet lag but without making it in any sense better. The water in the toilets is not usually treated, but there is usually a dispenser just outside the toilet door: asking the stewards to bring water to your seat usually results in a small plastic beaker that contains a bit of water with a lot of ice and they seem to be strangely reluctant to bring a litre bottle of mineral water and leave it for you to drink at will, but this is the answer. Insist upon it.

4. Exercise. When not otherwise engaged by being asleep or drinking water, take exercise. Walk about, stretch, wriggle your toes. Get off the plane at stopovers and take a walk.

Seize the chance of a shower if available during stopovers or if available in First Class. A shower is not only refreshing but it also improves circulation.

5. When flying west, you are lengthening your day, so it is best, if possible, to avoid sleeping on the plane; this will jeopardise your chances of a decent night's sleep once you arrive.

6. The opposite applies when flying east, especially overnight, so eat as little as possible and try to get as much sleep as possible.

Taking medication to fight jet lag is a controversial issue. Conventional sleeping tablets are not recommended while travelling for the reasons shown above, but they can help restore sleep patterns on arrival.

Homeopathy and Aromatherapy

Various homeopathic remedies are recommended for jet lag's various symptoms. Arnica is recommended for sleeplessness, restlessness, mental strain and shock. Bellis Perennis, extracted from the common daisy, is suggested to alleviate venous congestion due to *mechanicla auses* and waking mid-sleep. Chamomilla is prescribed to alleviate emotional and mental stress, sleeplessness, impatience, intolerance and disorientation while Ipecacuanha is thought to help minimise the effects of dehydration.

Leading aromatherapist Valerie Ann Worwood suggests two treatments for swollen feet and ankles but they do need preparing in advance. Damp a small piece of cotton with water and add five drops of lavender essential oil: place in a plastic bag and apply this as a compress, as well as massaging your feet in an upwards motion during and after the journey. Alternatively, massage with an oil made from lavender or eucalyptus essential oil and massage oil, mixed in a proportion of five drops to one teaspoon. On arrival, restore your body's timeclock by using peppermint and eucalyptus essential oils in morning baths and lavender and geranium in the evenings, either in the bath or applied with a face cloth. To revitalise after a long flight, she suggests a long soak in a hot bath tanged with the aroma of grapefruit oil.

Melatonin

Personally, I always use Melatonin, which is the seratonin that tells the body's Circadian Rhythm that it's time for bed. A 3mg tablet taken on the plane makes it much easier to go to sleep, and Melatonin, which influences the body's hormones, can be used in the same way as a sleeping pill to reset sleep patterns to a new time zone without the residual doziness. Note that Melatonin does not work for everyone, especially if carbohydrate is consumed after taking the tablet. Until recently Melatonin was available over the counter in the UK and can still be easily bought in America or mail-order over the internet: most doctors are quite aware of Melatonin and are generally prepared to write a private prescription.

FLYING IN COMFORT

by Richard Harrington

Flying is physically a lot more stressful than many people realise. And there is more to the problem than time zones. Modern jet aircraft are artificially pressurised at an altitude pressure of around 1500 to 2000 metres. That means that when you are flying at an altitude of, say, 12,000 metres in a Boeing 747, the cabin pressure inside is what it would be if you were outside at a height of 1500 to 2000 metres above sea level. Most people live a lot closer to sea level than this, and to be rocketed almost instantly to a height of 2000 metres (so far as their body is concerned) takes a considerable amount of adjustment. Fortunately, the human body is a remarkably adaptable organism, and for most individuals the experience is stressful, but not fatal.

Although it might seem more practical to pressurise the cabin to sea level pressure, this is currently impossible. A modern jet with sea level cabin pressure would have to have extremely strong (and therefore heavy) outside walls to prevent the difference between inside and outside walls causing the aircraft walls to rupture in mid-flight. At present, there is no economically viable lightweight material that is strong enough to do the job. Another problem is that if there were a rupture at, say, 14,000 metres, with an interior pressure equal to that at sea level, there would be no chance for the oxygen masks to drop in the huge sucking process that would result from the air inside the cabin emptying through the hole in the aircraft. A 2000 metres equivalent pressure at least gives passengers and oxygen masks a chance if this occurs.

Inside the cabin, humidifiers and fragrance disguise all the odours of large numbers of people in a confined space. On a long flight you are breathing polluted air.

Surviving the Onslaught

What can you do to help your body survive the onslaught? First, you can loosen your clothing. The body swells in the thinner air of the cabin, so take off your shoes (wear loose shoes anyway, it can be agony putting tight ones back on at the end of the flight), undo your belt, tilt your seat right back, put a couple of pillows in the lumbar region of your back and one behind your neck, and whether you are trying to sleep or simply rest, cover your eyes with a pair of air travel blinkers (ask the stewardess for a pair if you have not brought any with you).

Temperatures rise and fall notoriously inside an aircraft, so have a blanket ready over your knees in case you nod off and later find that you are freezing. When I look at all the space wasted over passengers' heads in a Boeing 747, and all those half-empty hand baggage lockers, I often wonder why aircraft manufacturers do not arrange things so that comfortable hammocks can be slung over our heads for those who want to sleep – or better still, small couchettes in tiers like those found in modern submarines. Personally, I would prefer such comfort, whatever it might do to the tidiness of the cabin interior. However, if you do not mind paying, you can actually lie down in a bed in some airlines' First Class sections. BA will even tuck you up in a "comfort suit", with hot chocolate and biscuits to complete the experience.

On a long flight it is tempting to feel you are not getting your money's worth if you do not eat and drink everything that is going. Stop and resist the temptation – even if you are travelling in First Class and all that food and drink seems to be what most of the extra cost is about. Most people find it best to eat lightly before leaving home and little or nothing during the flights. Foods that are too rich or spicy and foods that you are unaccustomed to will do little to make you feel good in flight. Neither will alcohol. Some people claim that they travel better if they drink fizzy drinks in flight, although if inclined to indigestion, the gas can cause discomfort as it is affected by the lower pressure in the cabin. Tea and coffee are diuretics (increase urine output) and so have the undesirable effect of further dehydrating the drinker who is already in the very dry atmosphere of the cabin. Fruit juices and plain water are best.

Smoking raises the level of carbon monoxide in the blood (and, incidentally, in the atmosphere, so that non-smokers can also suffer the ill effects if seated close to smokers) and reduces the smoker's tolerance to altitude. A smoker is already effectively at 1500 to 2000 metres before leaving the ground.

Walk up and down as frequently as possible during a flight to keep your circulation in shape, and do not resist the urge to go to the loo (avoid the queues by going before meals). The time will pass more quickly, and you will feel better for it, if you get well into an unputdownable novel before leaving home and try to finish it during the flight. This trick always works better than flicking half-heartedly through an in-flight magazine.

It may be worth trying to find out how full a 'plane is before you book, or, given the circumstances, choosing to fly in the low season to increase your chance of getting empty seats to stretch out on for a good sleep. If you have got a choice of seats on a 'plane, remember there is usually more leg room by the emergency exit over the wings. On the other hand, stewardesses tend to gather at the tail end of the 'plane on most airlines, so they try not to give seats there away unless asked. That means you may have more chance of ending up with empty seats next to you if you go for the two back rows (also statistically the safest place in a crash). Seats in the middle compartment over the forward part of the wing are said to give the smoothest ride; the front area of the 'plane is, however, the quietest.

If possible, take your own pillow, which will be a useful supplement to the postage-stamp sized pillows supplied by most airlines.

Finally, if you plan to sleep during the flight, put a "Do Not Disturb" notice by your seat and pass up the chance of another free drink or face towel every time your friendly neighbourhood stewardess comes round. You probably will not arrive at the other end raring to go, but if you have planned it wisely to arrive just before nightfall, and if you take a brisk walk before going to bed, you might just get lucky and go straight to sleep without waking up on home time two hours later.

Chapter Three
STRESS, FOOD, BUGS AND BITES

DAY TO DAY SURVIVAL: GENERAL HEALTH PROBLEMS ABROAD

by Dr Nick Beeching

It goes without saying that travellers should always seek qualified medical attention if any illness they are suffering from gets worse despite their own remedies, or, for that matter any of those mentioned so far in this book! But finding and dealing with doctors in a foreign country can be a daunting task. This article will help you to locate a doctor and, with a bit of background knowledge, to get the best out of him or her once you have fallen ill. So far we have spoken only about prevention of disease and illness. This chapter is for those of you who are already ill or are in need of medication or qualified medical attention. We will also deal with more everyday problems such as food and water and coming to terms with culture shock.

Large hotels usually have access to doctors, typically a local family doctor or private clinic. In more remote areas, the nearest qualified help will be a rural dispensary or pharmacist, but seek advice from local expatriate groups, your consulate or embassy for details of local doctors. In large towns, university-affiliated hospitals should be used in preference to other hospitals. In remote areas, mission hospitals usually offer excellent care and often have English-speaking doctors. The International Association for Medical

Assistance to Travellers (IAMAT) produces an invaluable directory of English-speaking doctors (see the directory at the back of this book for their address).

If you feel that your medical condition is deteriorating despite (or because of) local medical attention, consider travelling home or to a city or country with more advanced medical expertise – sooner rather than later.

Medication

Medicines sold in tropical pharmacies may be sub-standard. Always check the expiry date and check that medications that should have been refrigerated are not being sold on open shelves. There is a growing market in counterfeit drugs and locally-prepared substitutes are often of low potency. Stick to brand names manufactured by large international companies, even if these cost more. Insist on buying bottles that have unbroken seals and, wherever possible, purchase tablets or capsules that are individually sealed in foil or plastic wrappers. It is difficult to adulterate or substitute the contents of such packaging.

It is usually wise to avoid medications that include several active pharmacological ingredients, most of which will be ineffective and will push up the cost. Medication that is not clearly labelled with the pharmacological name as well as the brand name of ingredients is suspect (e.g. *Nivaquine* contains chloroquine).

Fevers

Fever may herald a number of exotic infections, especially when accompanied by a rash. Fever in a malarious area should be investigated by blood tests, even if you are taking antimalarials. A raised temperature is more commonly due to virus infections such as influenza, or localised bacterial infections that have obvious localising features such as middle ear infections or sinusitis, urinary tract infections (pain or blood passing water), skin infections or chest infections including pneumonia (cough, chest pain or shortness of breath).

If medical attention is not available, the best antibiotic for amateurs is cotrimoxazole (*Bactrim* or *Septrin*) which contains a sulphur drug, and trimethoprim. This covers all the above bacterial infections as well as typhoid fever. Travellers who are allergic to sulphur drugs could use trimethoprim alone or coamoxyclav (*Augmentin*) which is a combined oral penicillin preparation.

Local Infections

Athlete's Foot: Can become very florid in the tropics so treat this problem before departure. The newer antifungal creams e.g. *Canesten*, are very effective and supersede antifungal dusting powders, but do not eliminate the need for sensible foot hygiene. In very moist conditions, e.g. in rain forests, on cave explorations or in small boats, lacerated feet can become a real and incapacitating problem. A silicon-based barrier cream in adequate supply is essential under these conditions.

In muddy or wet conditions, most travellers will get some skin sepsis or small wounds. Without sensible hygiene these can be disabling, especially in jungle conditions. Cuts and grazes should be washed thoroughly with soap and water or an antiseptic solution.

Large abrasions should be covered with a vaseline gauze, e.g. *Jelonet* or *Sofratulle*, then a dry gauze, and kept covered until a dry scab forms, after which they can be left exposed. Anchor dressings are useful for awkward places (e.g. fingers or heels). If a cut is clean and gaping, bring the edges together with *Steristrips* in place of stitches.

Blisters: Burst with a sterile blade or needle (boiled for three minutes or held in a flame until red hot). Remove dead skin. Cover the raw area with zinc oxide plaster and leave in place for several days to allow new skin to form.

Ears: Keep dry with a light plug of cotton wool but don't poke matches in. If there is discharge and pain, take an antibiotic.

Eyes: If the eyes are pink and feel gritty, wear dark glasses and put in chloromycetin ointment or drugs. Seek medical attention if relief is not rapid or if a foreign body is present in the eye.

Feet: Feet take a hammering so boots must fit and be comfortable. Climbing boots are rarely necessary on the approach march to a mountain; trainers are useful. At the first sign of rubbing put on a plaster.

Sinusitis: Gives a headache (feels worse on stooping), "toothache" in the upper jaw, and often a thick, snotty discharge from the nose. Inhale steam or sniff a tea brew with a towel over your head to help drainage. Decongestant drops may clear the nose if it is mildly bunged up, but true sinusitis needs an antibiotic so seek advice.

Teeth: When it is difficult to brush your teeth, chew gum. If a filling comes out, a plug of cotton wool soaked in oil of cloves eases the pain; *gutta percha*, softened in boiling water, is easily plastered into the hole as a temporary filling. Hot salt mouth-washes encourage pus to discharge from a dental abscess but an antibiotic will be needed.

Throat: Cold dry air irritates the throat and makes it sore. Gargle with a couple of aspirins or table salt dissolved in warm water, or suck antiseptic lozenges.

Unconsciousness

The causes range from drowning to head injury, diabetes to epilepsy. Untrained laymen should merely attempt to place the victim in the coma position – lying on their side with the head lower than the chest to allow secretions, blood or vomit to drain away from the lungs. Hold the chin forward to prevent the tongue falling back and obstructing the airway. Don't try any fancy manoeuvres unless you are practised, as you may do more harm than good. *All unconscious patients, from any cause, particularly after trauma, should be placed in the coma position until they recover. This takes priority over any other first aid manoeuvre.* Fainting: lay the unconscious person down and raise the legs to return extra blood to the brain.

Injury

Nature is a wonderful healer if given adequate encouragement.

Burns: Superficial burns are simply skin wounds. Leave open to the air to form a dry crust under which healing goes on. If this is not possible, cover with *Melolin* dressings. Burn creams offer no magic. Deep burns must be kept scrupulously clean and treated urgently by a doctor. Give drinks freely to replace lost fluids.

Deep wounds: Firm pressure on a wound dressing will stop most bleeding. If blood seeps through, put more dressings on top, secured with absorbent crepe bandages and keep up the pressure. Elevate the injured part if possible.

On trips to remote spots at least one member of the party should learn to put in simple sutures. This is not difficult – a friendly doctor or casualty sister can teach the essentials in ten minutes. People have practised on a piece of dog meat and on several occasions this has been put to good use. Pulling the wound edges together is all that is necessary, a neat cosmetic result is usually not important.

Fractures: Immobilise the part by splinting to a rigid structure; the arm can be strapped to the chest, both legs can be tied together. Temporary splints can be made from a rolled newspaper, an ice-axe or a branch. Pain may be agonising and is due to movement of broken bone ends on each other; full doses of strong pain killers are needed.

The aim of splinting fractures is to reduce pain and bleeding at the fracture site and thereby to reduce shock. Comfort is the best criterion by which to judge the efficiency of a splint but remember that to immobilise a fracture when the victim is being carried, splints may need to be tighter than seems necessary for comfort when at rest, particularly over rough ground. Wounds at a fracture site or visible bones must be covered immediately with sterile, or the cleanest, material available and if this happens, start antibiotic treatment at once. Pneumatic splints provide excellent support but may be inadequate when a victim with a broken leg has a difficult stretcher ride across rough ground. They are of no value for fractured femurs (thigh bones). If you decide to take them, get the *Athletic Long* splint which fits over a climbing boot where the *Standard Long Leg* splint does not.

Sprains: A sprained ankle ligament, usually on the outside of the joint, is a common and likely injury. With broad *Elastoplast* "stirrup strapping", walking may still be possible. Put two or three long lengths from mid-calf on the non-injured side, attach along the calf on the injured side. Follow this with circular strapping from toes to mid-calf overlapping by half on each turn. First aid treatment of sprains and bruises is: immobilisation (I); cold, e.g. cold compresses (C); and elevation (E); *remember ICE*. If painful movement and swelling persist, suspect a fracture.

Swimming (see also Marine Bites)

Freshwater swimming is not advisable when crocodiles or hippopotamuses are in the vicinity. Beware of polluted water as it is almost impossible to avoid swallowing some. Never dive into water of unknown depth. Broken necks caused by careless diving are a far greater hazard to travellers than crocodiles.

Lakes, ponds, reservoirs, dams, slow streams and irrigation ditches may harbour bilharzia (schistosomiasis). This is a widespread infection in Africa, the Middle East and parts of the Far East and South America, and is a genuine hazard for swimmers. (See *Bilharzia* article in Chapter Four.)

Scuba Diving

Scuba divers should be sure that local instruction and equipment is adequate and should always swim with a partner. Do not fly within three hours of diving, or within 24 hours of any dive requiring a decompression stop on the way back to the surface. Travellers who anticipate scuba diving in their travels are strongly advised to have proper training before setting out.

Snorkelling

(by Jack Barker)

Snorkelling is a great way to see the seabed, provided that a proper mask is used, enclosing the nose. Eye-goggles can cause bruising and eye damage from the pressure of water. A more serious risk is the practice of hyperventilating (taking several deep breaths) before diving, in the hope of extending a dive. This can kill. Normally, the lungs tell the body to surface for air when the carbon dioxide level is too high. Hyperventilation disrupts this mechanism, so the body can run out of oxygen before the lungs send out their danger signals. This can lead to underwater blackouts, and drowning.

Drowning seems rather too obvious a risk to mention here but it is simultaneously the most common and the most serious risk of any watersport, and in many cases alcohol is involved. Don't swim drunk. Some authorities still maintain that swimming after meals runs a risk of stomach cramps although this is now a minority view. In the sea and rivers, watch out for tides and rips: even a current of one knot is usually enough to exhaust most swimmers quickly. Swimming directly against a strong current is especially exhausting, and, if possible, it is best to swim across the flow, and so gradually make your way to the shore.

Safe swimmers find local advice before taking to the water. Deserted beaches are often deserted for a reason, whether it be sharks, invisible jellyfish, or vicious rip tides. Try to swim in pairs: a friend nearby in the water is more likely to distinguish between waving and drowning.

GETTING STUNG ON LAND AND IN THE WATER

Mammalian Bites

(by Dr Nick Beeching)

All mammalian bites (including human ones) are likely to become infected, and medical advice should be obtained about appropriate antibiotics and tetanus immunisation. First aid measures start with immediate washing of the wound in running water for at least five minutes, scrubbing with soap or detergent, and removal of any obvious imbedded foreign material. Wiping with topical iodine, an alcohol injection swab or neat alcohol (gin or whisky will do) helps to sterilise the area. Colourful topical agents such as mercurochrome are useless. At the hospital or dispensary the wound should be cleaned and dressed again, but do not allow the wound to be sutured.

Rabies is a serious hazard throughout most of the world, including continental Europe and the USA. Domestic or wild animal contact should be avoided at all times, particularly if a normally wild animal is unusually docile or vice versa. Rabies affects a wide variety of mammals, particularly carnivores and bats. Wild dogs are a common nuisance in the tropics and should be given a wide berth. (See the article on rabies in Chapter Four.)

Snakes

Snakes only attack humans if provoked and snakebite is a rare hazard for most travellers. Never handle a snake, even if it appears to be dead, and try not to corner or threaten live snakes. If you encounter a snake on the path, keep absolutely still until it moves away. Always look for snakes on paths ahead, using a torch at night. If hiking on overgrown paths, through undergrowth or sand, wear adequate boots, socks and long trousers. Snakes are often found in wood piles, crevices or under rocks and these should not be handled. Integral groundsheets and tightly closed tent flaps help to keep snakes out of tents, and make it less likely that you will roll over on a snake in your sleep – generally viewed as threatening behaviour by the snake.

Not all snakes are venomous and only a minority of bites by venomous species are accompanied by a successful injection of venom. The most important first aid for a victim is to keep calm and provide reassurance that envenomation is unlikely. Immobilise the bitten limb by splinting and rest the victim.

Do not offer alcohol. Even if venom has been injected, severe effects take several hours to develop and there should be adequate time to carry the patient to a dispensary or hospital for trained help. A tight tourniquet around the thigh or upper arm is only recommended for bites by cobras, kraits, coral snakes, sea snakes and most Australian snakes. Usually, it is best to apply a tight pressure dressing over the bite or crepe bandaging on the affected limb (which should be immobilised).

"Boys' Own" remedies such as incision of the wound to suck out the venom are harmful and should not be employed. Local sprays, cold packs, topical antiseptics and even electric shocks are equally useless.

If the snake has already been killed, place it in a bag or box and take it for identification by medical staff attending the victim. Amateur attempts to capture a snake that has been provoked may result in further bites and a good description of the snake by an unbitten comrade is preferable.

Depending on the type of snake, venom may reduce the clotting activity of the blood, causing bleeding, typically from the gums, or induce paralysis – first manifested by an inability to open the eyes properly, followed by breathing problems. Shock and kidney failure are also possibilities and some venoms cause extensive damage to tissue around the bitten area. Immediate pain relief should never include aspirin, which impairs the ability of blood to clot. All bites, with or without envenomation, carry a risk of infection.

Antivenom should never be used unless there are definite signs of envenomation, and then only with adequate medical support. Travellers should not routinely carry antivenom. Expatriates working in high-risk remote areas or expedition organisers may wish to carry a small stock of antivenom. British travellers who wish to carry antivenom should obtain specialist advice from the WHO Centre at the Liverpool School of Tropical Medicine several months before they intend to travel. Package inserts with multi-purpose antivenoms and even local advice are often incorrect.

Scorpions

Scorpion stings are far more likely to be a problem for travellers and are always very painful. Scorpions are widespread, particularly in hot dry areas. If travelling in such areas wear strong footwear and always shake out your clothes and shoes before putting them on. The pain of stings requires medical attention, which may include strong, injected pain-killers. Many species are capable of inflicting fatal stings, particularly in children, and antivenoms should be available in areas where these species are present.

Other Beasts

A myriad of other stinging and biting beasts threaten the traveller. Some spider bites can cause rapid paralysis and should be treated with a local pressure dressing or tight tourniquet until medical help is obtained. Leeches can be encouraged to drop off by applying salt, alcohol or vinegar or a lighted cigarette end. Do not pull them off, as infection may follow if parts of the mouth remain in the wound. Leeches inject an anticoagulant into the wound and local pressure may be required to reduce bleeding. If travelling in damp jungle areas through water with leeches, inspect all exposed areas regularly for leeches.

Marine Bites and Other Sea Stings

(by Jack Barker)

The temptation to explore below the surface of a blue tropical sea can be irresistible. But be warned: it's an environment designed for fish, and it's a survival game even for them. Behind the postcard image of a coral reef is a festering soup of malevolent life. With sea-urchins snapping around heels, stonefish lurking in the shallows, coral waiting to inflict highly infective scrapes and sharks and jellyfish patrolling the deep it is quite surprising that the most common after-effect of subaquatic exploration is an ear infection, which can strike even from the smallest paddling pool. On this and other matters, medical advice is divided.

Ear Infections

Ear infections are caused by the residue of water that hangs around in the outer canal of the ear, waiting to cause what the doctors casually refer to as an "indolent infection", either fungal or bacterial.

Indolent it may be, but it certainly hurts, and can take months to shift. The Medical Advisory Service for Travellers Abroad (MASTA) recommends drying ears with a cotton bud, gently pulling the lobe of the ear back and inserting a the bud to soak up remaining water. They caution not to twist the bud, and to take care not to poke it through the eardrum (causing pain and irreparable deafness).

Surgeon Lieutenant Commander Simon Ridout, who looks after navy divers, disagrees. He says the only safe way to get water out of the ear is by shaking your head like a dog. In practice I find this makes my brain feel as if it is coming loose, but it is easy to see it avoids the risk of inducing infection thought to be caused by microscopic cotton fragments left by even a sterile cotton bud. He also warns that diving or swimming with a cold or sore throat increases the risks of such infections.

Sea Urchins

Sea urchins are vicious little balls of spines that spend their days in rock crevices waiting for an unwary foot. Nocturnal skinny-dippers should be warned that at night they also travel across open sand. Swimming shoes should be worn where sea urchins are found. Spines should be methodically removed after softening the skin in a two per cent salycilic solution. Be careful not to leave any remnants of spine in the wound.

Jellyfish

Jellyfish trail tentacles armed with stinging capsules. To make matters worse, many species are invisible. MASTA suggest washing the wound with vinegar or dilute acetic acid, which neutralises the venom in the tentacles which are probably still wrapped around the victim. The Surf

Lifesaving Association of Australia no longer recommend this treatment, however, and now suggest washing in plenty of ice and cold water. Once the jellyfish has been removed, all fragments of tentacle should be picked off the surface of the patient's skin. An itchy or painful rash is the usual result of a jellyfish sting, but some species are venomous enough to kill and allergic reactions can also complicate matters. If the patient becomes short of breath, starts to sweat, or shows signs of inflammation spreading from the sting, they should be taken to hospital and given cardiac massage and mouth-to-mouth respiration on the way if necessary.

Fish

Fish can cause a certain amount of havoc: stingrays, weeverfish, and scorpionfish are all equipped to kill humans. Most stings occur when the fish has been surprised, so shuffle along the seabed to warn the unsuspecting of your presence. If stung by any of the above, the sting should be removed, the wound bound tightly, the limb immobilised and the patient taken to hospital. Cardiac massage and artificial respiration should be used if the patient stops breathing. If this is not convenient (or possible) the poison from these fish can be destroyed by heat, so the excruciating pain and some of the worst toxic effects can be relieved by immersing the bite in hot, but not scalding, water (about 50°C).

Sharks

Sharks present less of a risk than is generally thought. There are about 100 recorded attacks each year, which is dwarfed by the drowning figures. Conventional wisdom states that the best policy is to sit on the seabed quietly until any prowling shark goes away, although this would clearly be difficult without breathing apparatus. As with all sea risks, it is best to take local advice. In high-risk areas such as Sydney, popular beaches are netted, although it has been suggested that sharks caught inside the nets are more, not less, likely to resort to crunching humans for food.

Coral

Coral does not have to be venomous to cause medical problems. Even minor coral scrapes can develop into tropical ulcers and take months to heal, and should be disinfected immediately. In Belize my boatman treated cuts with a spray of an aerosol window-cleaner containing ammonia, which seemed to work perfectly, but the conventional advice is to use a zinc medication or a powder such as Cicatrin.

INJECTIONS AND BLOOD TRANSFUSIONS

by Drs Sharon Welby and Nick Beeching

Many diseases are spread by blood, blood products and instruments which may be contaminated with blood. When travelling in developing countries it is vitally important to be aware of the potential risks associated with having injections or blood transfusions.

In some countries the health care facilities are under tremendous financial strain. Equipment may be reused without proper sterilisation and there may be no formal programme for screening donated blood for antibodies to HIV or hepatitis B or C. It is, therefore, a wise precaution to take a commercially prepared HIV prevention kit when travelling to tropical and sub-tropical destinations. The HIV prevention kit usually contains syringes, needles, intravenous cannulae and sometimes a dental needle and suture kit. They are available from most large chemists, camping shops and travel clinics, and the advantage of a commercial kit is that all the items are clearly labelled and you are unlikely to run into problems at customs. It is wise to keep these kits on you at all times because they will do you little good if left behind in your hotel. Bigger packs containing plasma expander solutions are of limited use, are inconvenient to carry and are probably not necessary unless travelling as part of an expedition where medical help is available.

The risk associated with unscreened blood transfusions is significant given the high prevalence of HIV and hepatitis B infection in tropical countries. Blood transfusions can also transmit other viruses (hepatitis C, D and cytomegalovirus); bacteria (syphilis and meliodosis); and parasites (including filariasis "elephantiasis", visceral leishmaniasis, trypanosomiasis – sleeping sickness in Africa and Chagas' disease in the Americas – and malaria).

If you are in the unfortunate position of needing a blood transfusion, ask the attending doctors whether the transfusion is absolutely necessary to save life (in which case there is little choice). If transfusion is essential but can be deferred for a short period, members of your own party, local expatriates, or donors who know their own HIV and hepatitis B status may be able to donate blood for you. The embassy or consulate staff can often help with information about local donors. Establishing your blood group before travelling is a sensible precaution and there is a charitable organisation which guarantees to supply screened blood within 24 hours to members. Enquiries can be made through the Medical Advisory Service for Travellers Abroad, tel: 0113-239 1700 (fees start from £7.50 per month).

As with everything, prevention is better than cure when it comes to blood transfusions. The majority of transfusions are the result of accidents, road accidents in particular, so be aware that the risk of road accidents can be reduced by taking simple precautions: not travelling at night, not getting on overcrowded vehicles, avoiding motorcycles and not drinking and driving.

The risk of diseases spread by injections can be prevented by avoiding unnecessary injections and needles, for example, acupuncture, body or ear piercing and tattoos. It is also advisable not to share razors, so don't be tempted to have your face shaved in the street. Hepatitis B and C may also be transmitted by sharing toothbrushes, nail scissors and other items which can cause bleeding, and individuals should only use their own toiletry items.

If you do become unwell and the health care professional intends to give you an injection, question if it is really necessary and if there is an alternative treatment. Sometimes the injection or infusion is seen as a modern and more effective treatment when in reality a tablet will be as effective. If the injection is essential, make sure a disposable needle is opened in front of you.

Drug users who share needles, syringes and other drug-injecting paraphernalia also share a large number of infections, including hepatitis B, HIV, malaria and some exotic diseases such as Chagas' disease found in South America. The risk of acquiring hepatitis or HIV is substantially increased if your partner is an injecting drug user. Intravenous drug users, who are not deterred by the serious legal consequences of their habit, should not share "works" or "mixing spoons" under any circumstances. To share is to invite disaster.

CULTURE SHOCK
by Adrian Furnham

Nearly every traveller must have experienced culture shock at some time or other. Like jet lag, it is an aspect of travel which is both negative and difficult to define. But what precisely is it? When and why does it occur? And, more importantly, how can we prevent it or at least cope with it?

Although the experience of culture shock has no doubt been around for centuries, it was only 30 years ago that an anthropologist called Oberg coined the term. Others have attempted to improve upon and extend the concept and have come up with alternative jargon such as "culture fatigue", "role shock" and "pervasive ambiguity".

Strain

From the writings of travellers and interviews with tourists, foreign students, migrants and refugees, psychologists have attempted to specify the exact nature of this unpleasant experience. It seems that the syndrome has five facets. Firstly, there is strain caused by the effort of making necessary psychological adaptations – speaking another language, coping with the currency, driving on the other side of the road, etc. Secondly, there is often a sense of loss and a feeling of deprivation with regard to friends, possessions and status. If you are in a place where nobody knows, loves, respects and confides in you, you may feel anonymous and deprived of your status and role in society, as well as bereft of familiar and useful objects. Thirdly, there is often a feeling of rejection – your rejection of the natives and their rejection of you. Travellers stand out by their skin, clothes, and language. Depending on the experience of the natives, they may be seen as unwanted intruders, an easy rip-off, or friends.

A fourth symptom of culture shock is confusion. Travellers can become unsure about their roles, their values, their feelings and sometimes about who they are. When a people lives by a different moral and social code from your own, interaction for even a comparatively short period can be very confusing. Once one becomes more aware of cultural differences, typical reactions of surprise, anxiety, even disgust and indignation occur. The way foreigners treat their animals, eat food, worship their god, or perform their toiletries often cause amazement and horror to naïve travellers. Finally, culture shock often involves feelings of impotence due to not being able to cope with the new environment.

Little England

Observers of sojourners and long-term travellers have noted that there are usually two extreme reactions to culture shock: those who act as if they "never left home" and those who immediately "go native". The former chauvinists create "little Englands" in foreign fields, refusing to compromise their diet or dress, and like the proverbial mad dogs, insisting on going out in the midday sun. The latter reject all aspects of their own culture and enthusiastically do in Rome as the Romans do.

Most travellers, however, experience less dramatic but equally uncomfortable reactions to culture shock. These may include excessive concern over drinking water, food, dishes and bedding; fits of anger over delays and other minor frustrations; excessive fear of being cheated, robbed or injured; great concern over minor pains and interruptions; and a longing to be back at the idealised home "where you can get a good cup of tea and talk to sensible people".

But, as any seasoned traveller will know, often one begins to get used to, and even learns to like the new culture. In fact writers have suggested that people go through a number of phases when living in a new culture. Oberg, in his original writings, listed four stages: the "honeymoon" which is characterised by enchantment, fascination, enthusiasm and admiration for the new culture as well as cordial (but superficial) relationships. In this stage people are generally intrigued and euphoric. Many tourists never stay long enough to move out of the honeymoon period. The second phase heralds crisis and disintegration. It is now that the traveller feels loss, isolation, loneliness and inadequacy, and tends to become depressed and withdrawn. This happens most often after two to six months of living in the new culture.

The third phase is the most problematic and involves rein-
tegration. At this point people tend to reject the host culture,
becoming opinionated and negative partly as a means of
showing their self-assertion and growing self-esteem. The
fourth stage of "autonomy" finds the traveller assured,
relaxed, warm and empathic because he or she is socially
and linguistically capable of negotiating most new and different social situations in the culture.

And finally the "independent" phase is achieved – characterised by trust, humour and the acceptance and enjoyment of social, psychological and cultural differences.

U-Curve

For obvious reasons, this independent phase is called the
"U-curve" hypothesis. If you plot satisfaction and adapta-
tion (x axis) over time (y axis), you see a high point beginning, followed by a steep decline, a period at the bottom, but
then a steady climb back up. More interestingly, some
researchers have shown evidence not of a U-curve but a "W-
curve", i.e. once travellers return to their home country, they
often undergo a similar re-acculturation, again in the shape
of a U. Hence a "double U" or W-curve.

Other research has shown similar intriguing findings.
Imagine, for instance, that you are going to Morocco for the
first time. You are asked to describe or rate both the average
Briton and the average Moroccan in terms of their humour,
wealth, trustworthiness etc., both before you go and after
you return. Frequently it has been found that people change
their opinions of their own countrymen and women more
than that of the foreigners. In other words, travel makes you
look much more critically at yourself and your culture than
most people think. And this self-criticism may itself be
rather unhelpful.

The trouble with these stage theories is that not everyone
goes through the stages. Not everyone feels like Nancy

Mitford when she wrote: "I loathe abroad, nothing would induce me to live there… and, as for foreigners, they are all the same and make me sick". But I suspect Robert Morley is not far from the truth when he remarked: "The British tourist is always happy abroad so long as the natives are waiters".

Then there is also the shock of being visited. Anyone who lives in a popular tourist town soon becomes aware that it is not only the tourist but also the native who experiences culture shock. Of course, the amount and type of shock that tourists can impart to local people is an indication of a number of things, such as the relative proportion of tourists to natives, the duration of their stay, the comparative wealth and development of the two groups and the racial and ethnic prejudices of both.

Of course not everybody will experience culture shock. Older, better educated, confident and skillful adults (particularly those who speak the language) tend to adapt best. Yet there is considerable evidence that some sojourners, like foreign students, voluntary workers, businessmen, diplomats and even military people, become so confused and depressed that they have to be sent home at great expense. That is why many organisations attempt to lessen culture shock by a number of training techniques. The Foreign Office, the British Council and many multi-nationals do this for good reason, learning from bitter experience.

Training

For a number of reasons, information and advice in the form of lectures and pamphlets, etc., is very popular but not always very useful. The "facts" that are given are often too general to have any clear, specific application in particular circumstances. Facts emphasise the exotic and ignore the mundane (how to hail a taxi, for example). This technique also gives the impression that the culture can be easily understood; and even if facts are retained, they do not necessarily lead to accommodating behaviour.

A second technique is "isomorphic training". This is based on the theory that a major cause of cross-cultural communication problems comes from the fact that most people tend to offer different explanations for each other's behaviour. This technique introduces various episodes that end in embarrassment, misunderstanding or hostility between people from two different cultures. The trainee is then presented with four or five alternative explanations of what went wrong, all of which correspond to different attributions of the observed behaviour. Only one is correct from the perspective of the culture being learned. This is an interesting and useful technique but depends for much of its success on the relevance of the various episodes chosen.

Perhaps the most successful method is "skills training". It has been pointed out that socially inadequate or inept individuals have not mastered the social conventions of their own society. Either they are unaware of the rules and processes of everyday behaviour or, if aware of the rules, they are unable or unwilling to abide by them. They are therefore like strangers in their own land. People newly arrived in an alien culture will be in a similar position and may benefit from simple skills training.

This involves analysing everyday encounters such as buying and selling, introductions, refusal of requests. You will also observe successful culture models engaging in these acts and will practise yourself, helped in the learning process by a video tape of your efforts. This may all sound very clinical, but can be great fun and very informative.

Practical Advice

Many travellers, unless on business and with considerable company resources behind them, do not have the time or money to go on courses that prevent or minimise culture shock. They have to leap in at the deep end and hope that they can swim. But there are some simple things they can do that may well prevent the shock and improve communications.

Before departure it is important to learn as much as possible about the society you are visiting. Areas of great importance include:

Language: Not only vocabulary but polite usage; when to use higher and lower forms; and particularly how to say "yes" and "no".

Non-verbal cues: Gestures, body contact, and eye gaze patterns differ significantly from one country to another and carry very important meanings. Cues of this sort for greeting, parting, and eating are most important, and are relatively easily learnt.

Social rules: Every society develops rules that regulate behaviour so that social goals can be attained and needs satisfied. Some of the most important rules concern gifts, buying and selling, eating and drinking, time keeping and bribery and nepotism.

Social relationships: Family relationships, classes and castes, and working relationships often differ from culture to culture. The different social roles of the two sexes is perhaps the most dramatic difference between societies, and travellers should pay special attention to this.

Motivation: Being assertive, extrovert and achievement-oriented may be desirable in America and Western Europe but this is not necessarily the case elsewhere. How to present oneself, maintain face, etc., is well worth knowing.

Once you have arrived, there are a few simple steps that you can take to help reduce perplexity and understand the natives:

Choose locals for friends: Avoid only mixing with compatriots or other foreigners. Get to know the natives who can introduce you to the subtleties and nuances of the culture.

Practical social activities: Do not be put off more complex social encounters but ask for information on appropriate etiquette. People are frequently happy to help and teach genuinely interested and courteous foreigners.

Avoid "good"/"bad" or "us"/"them" comparisons: Try to establish how and why people perceive and explain the same act differently, have different expectations, etc. Social behaviour has resulted from different historical and economic conditions and may be looked at from various perspectives.

When you return, the benefits of foreign travel and the prevention of the "W-curve" may be helped by the following:

Become more self-observant: Returning home makes one realise the comparative and normative nature of one's own behaviour which was previously taken for granted. This in turn may alert one to which behaviour is culturally at odds (and, perhaps, why) – in itself helpful for all future travel.

Helping the foreigner: There is no better teaching aid than personal experience. That is why many foreign language schools send their teachers abroad not only to improve their language but to experience the difficulties their students have. Remembering this, we should perhaps be in a better position to help the hapless traveller who comes to our country.

Travel does broaden the mind, but requires some effort. Preparation, it is said, prevents a pretty poor performance and travelling in different social environments is no exception. But this preparation may require social, as well as geographic maps.

FOOD ON THE MOVE
by Ingrid Cranfield

L iving a regular life, in one place most of the time, people get to know what foods they like and dislike and base a balanced diet on this rather than on text book nutrition. The problem is, how do you ensure you will have good food on the move? When travelling, you are constantly faced with new foods and it can be easy to lose track of how you are eating, simply because your rule of thumb menu-planning breaks down. This can lead to fatigue, a lack of energy and even poor health.

Essentially there are two ways of coping. You can either pick up local food as you travel, or you can take with you all your needs for the duration. Eating local food may give you a feeling of being closer to a country's way of life, but could also make you severely ill. Taking your own supplies is safe and very necessary if you are going into the wilds, but how do you stop your palate becoming jaded with endless supplies of dried food?

It is sensible to be able to recognise the constitution of all foods and to know what is necessary to keep you well fed. A balanced diet breaks down into six main areas: sugars, carbohydrates, fats, proteins, minerals/vitamins/salts and water – all are necessary, some in greater quantities than others.

Sugars: Technically called simple sugars, these are the simplest form of energy-stored-as-food. Because they are simple, the body finds them easy to absorb into the bloodstream – hence the term blood sugar. From here sugars are either turned directly to energy, or are stored as glycogen. The brain is very partial to using sugars for energy and if it is forced to run on other forms of food energy it complains by making you feel tired, headachy, and a bit wobbly-kneed.

Though it is important to have some sugars in your diet, try not to depend on them too much. Weight for weight they give you fewer calories than other food types. Also, if you take in lots of sugars at once, the body will react by over-producing insulin because your blood sugar is too high, so that in the end your blood sugar is taken down to a lower level than before. If you feel a desperate need for instant energy, try to take sugars with other food types to prevent this happening. While travelling, it is simple enough to recognise foods with lots of sugars – they are sweet. In less developed areas, sugar is still something of a luxury, so there will be less temptation!

Carbohydrates: Basically, carbohydrates are complex structures of simple sugars. Plants generally store energy as carbohydrate while animals store food energy as fat or glycogen. Carbohydrates have to be broken down into simple sugars by the body before they can be used as energy, so it takes longer to benefit from them after eating. Weight for weight, however, you will get three or four times more calories from carbohydrates than from sugars.

Carbohydrates are stodgy, starchy and very filling: breads in the Western world, mealies in Africa, rice in the East, etc. The majority of food energy comes from carbohydrates, so, when travelling, find the local equivalent and base a diet around it.

Fats: Next to carbohydrates, most of our energy comes from fats. Our bodies store energy as fat because it is the most efficient way to do so. Weight for weight, fats give you nearly three times the energy of carbohydrates, so they are an extremely efficient way of carrying food energy.

Fats, of course, are fatty, oily, creamy and sometimes congeal. Foods high in fat include butter, dairy foods, etc., although there are other high fat foods that are less well known, such as egg yolk or nut kernels. Fats are necessary now and again because one reclusive vitamin is generated from a fat and, more obviously, because without these concentrated doses of energy it would take a lot longer to eat all the food you need, as with cows or elephants.

Proteins: One of the most misunderstood types of food in the West is protein. Traditionally thought of as something essential, and the more the better, the truth is that for adults very little is needed each day and bodies in the West work very hard to convert unnecessary protein into urea so that it can be flushed away.

Protein is used to build and repair bodies, so children need plenty of it, as do adults recovering from injury. Otherwise, the amount of protein needed each day is small – maybe a small egg's worth. Other than that, protein cannot be readily used for energy, and the body does not bother converting it unless it is heading for a state of starvation. Those people on a red meat diet are using very little of the protein it contains, relying on the fat content which can be up to 45 per cent. When you are wondering where protein appears in your food, bear in mind that protein is for growth, so young mammals have protein-packed milk, unhatched chicks have their own supply in the meat of an egg and to help trees off to a good start there is a healthy package of protein in nuts.

Minerals, Vitamins and Salts: All of these are essential for all-round health and fitness. Most of them cannot be stored by the body and so they should be taken regularly, preferably daily. Ten days' shortage of Vitamin C, for instance, and you feel run-down, tired and lethargic – perhaps without knowing why.

In the normal diet, most of your minerals and vitamins come from fresh fruit and vegetables. If you feel that you may not get enough fresh food, take a course of multivitamin tablets with you for the duration of your travels. They do not weigh very much and can save you lots of trouble.

If you are getting your vitamins and minerals from fresh foods, remember that they are usually tucked away just under the skin, if not in the skin itself. Polished and refined foodstuffs have lost a lot, if not all, of their vitamins, minerals and dietary fibre.

As regards salts, there is little cause for concern. It is easier to take too much than too little, and if you do err on the low side your body tells you by craving salty foods. Do not take salt tablets, you could upset your stomach lining.

How Much?

Nutritionists have a term for the amount of food energy needed to keep a body ticking over – the basal metabolic rate. Take a man and put him in a room at ideal temperature, humidity, etc., and make sure he does no work at all except stay alive and he will use about 600kCal in a day. This is his basal metabolic rate.

Those of us who do not lie stock still in a room all day need energy over and above that basic amount, to work and to keep warm. For living and working in average conditions, our daily energy requirement rises to about 2500kCal. If you are going to be physically active (backpacking, say) in a temperate climate, your energy use will go up to around 3500kCal per day. If we do the same hard work in an extremely cold climate, our energy rate could go up to 5000kCal. To need more than this we would need to do an immense amount of work or have an incredibly fast metabolism. Sadly for women, they do not burn up nearly as much energy doing the same work as men.

A little experience will tell you whether you need a little more or a little less than the average. With this knowledge, you are ready to plan just how much food you need to take for the number of days you are travelling.

When you come to work out amounts of various foodstuffs that make up your calorie intake for the day, books for slimmers or the health conscious are invaluable. They list not only calories, but often protein and other nutritional breakdown. Nutritional information is also given on the packet.

Eating Local Food

In developing countries, canned, powdered and dried foods are usually safe to eat, provided they are made up with purified water. Staples such as flour and cooking oils are nearly always safe.

Meat, poultry, fish and shellfish should look and smell fresh and be thoroughly cooked, though not over-cooked, as soon as possible after purchasing. They should be eaten while still hot or kept continuously refrigerated after preparation. Eggs are safe enough if reasonably fresh and thoroughly cooked.

Milk may harbour disease-producing organisms (tuberculosis, brucellosis). The "pasteurised" label in underdeveloped countries should not be depended upon. For safety, if not ideal taste, boil the milk before drinking. (Canned or powdered milk may generally be used without boiling for drinking or in cooking).

Butter and margarine are safe unless obviously rancid. Margarine's keeping qualities are better than those of butter. Cheeses, especially hard and semi-hard varieties, are normally quite safe; soft cheeses are not so reliable.

Vegetables for cooking are safe if boiled for a short time. Do check, though, that on fruit or vegetables the skin or peel is intact. Wash them thoroughly and peel them yourself if you plan to eat them raw.

Moist or cream pastries should not be eaten unless they have been continuously refrigerated. Dry baked goods, such as bread and cakes, are usually safe even without refrigeration.

Always look for food that is as fresh as possible. If you

can watch livestock being killed and cooked or any other food being prepared before you eat it, so much the better. Do not be deceived by plush surroundings and glib assurances. Often the large restaurant with its questionable standard of hygiene and practice of cooking food ahead of time is a less safe bet than the wayside vendor from whom you can take food cooked on an open fire, without giving flies or another person the chance to contaminate it. Before preparing bought food, always wash your hands in water that has been chlorinated or otherwise purified.

In restaurants, the same rules apply for which foods are safe to eat. Restaurants buy their food from shops just as you would. It is wise to avoid steak tartare and other forms of raw meat in the tropics as there is a risk of tapeworm. Fruit juice is safe if pressed in front of you. Protect freshly bought meat from flies and insects with a muslin cover.

Meat that is just "on the turn" can sometimes be saved by washing it in strong salty water. If this removes the glistening appearance and sickly sweet smell, the meat is probably safe to eat. Cold or half-warmed foods may have been left standing and are therefore a risk. Boil such meats and poultry for at least ten minutes to destroy bacteria before serving. Remember that hot spices and chillies do not sterilise meat. Ice-cream is especially to be avoided in all developing countries.

Rice and other grains and pulses will probably have preservatives added to them. These will need to be removed by thorough washing as they are indigestible.

Eating in developed countries is not entirely hazard-free. You should remember that Delhi Belly is no respecter of language and is just as likely to strike in Spain as in India. The rules for avoiding tummy trouble are much as above: stick to foods that are simple and hygienically prepared, and as close as possible to those you know and love – at least until your digestive system slowly adapts to change.

Off the Beaten Track

There is no right menu for a camping trip, because we all have slightly different tastes in food and there is an almost endless number of menu possibilities. So, what should you pack? Here are a few points you will want to consider when choosing the right foods: weight, bulk, cost per kg.

Obviously, water-weighted, tinned foods are out. So are most perishables – especially if you are going to be lugging your pantry on your back. You will want only lightweight, long-lasting, compact food. Some of the lightest, of course, are the freeze drieds. You can buy complete freeze dried meals that are very easily prepared: just add boiling water and wait five minutes. They have their drawbacks, however. First, they are very expensive. Second, even if you like these pre-packaged offerings, and many people do not, you can get tired of them very quickly.

A much more exciting and economical method is to buy dehydrated foods at the supermarket and combine them to create your own imaginative dinners. Dried beans, cereals, instant potato, meat bars, crackers, dry soup mixes, cocoa, pudding, gingerbread and instant cheesecake mixes are just a few of the possibilities. But do not forget to pack a few spices to make your creations possible.

Quantity and Palatability

Most people tend to work up a big appetite outdoors. About 0.9kg to 1.2kg of food per person per day is average. How much of which foods will make up that weight is up to you. You can guess pretty accurately about how much macaroni or cheese or how many pudding mixes you are likely to need.

Last, but not least, what do you like? If you do not care for instant butterscotch pudding or freeze dried stew at home, you will probably like it even less after two days on the trail. And if you have never tried something before, don't take the chance. Do your experimenting first. Do not shock your digestive system with a lot of strange or different new foods. Stick as closely as possible to what you are used to in order to avoid stomach upsets and indigestion. And make sure you pack a wide enough variety of foods to ensure you will not be subjected to five oatmeal breakfasts in a row or be locked into an inflexible plan.

Packaging Your Food

After purchasing your food, the next step is to re-package it. Except for freeze dried meals or other specially-sealed foods, it is a good idea to store supplies and spices in small freezer bags. Just pour in your pudding powder, salt or gingerbread mix, drop an identifying label in, to take all the guesswork (and fun) out of it, and tie a loose knot. Taking plastic into the wilderness may offend one's sensibilities but it works well. Out in the wilds you learn just how handy these lightweight, flexible, recyclable, moisture-proof bags really are.

Preparing Great Meals

Although cooking over an open fire is great fun, many areas do not allow and cannot support campfires, so don't head off without a stove. When choosing a stove, remember that the further off the beaten track you go, the more important size, weight and reliability become. Aside from a stove, you will also need a collapsible water container, means of water purification and a heavy bag in which to store your soot-bottomed pans. You will need individual eating utensils: spoon, cup and bowl will do. Also take a few recipes with you, or learn them before you leave. You can even have such luxuries as fresh baked bread if you are prepared to make the effort. Here are some tips about camp cooking, learned the hard way.

1. Cook on a low heat to avoid scorching.
2. Taste before salting (the bouillon cubes and powdered bases often added to camp casseroles are very salty: don't overdo it by adding more).
3. Add rice, pasta, etc., to boiling water to avoid sticky or slimy textures and add a knob of butter or margarine to stop the pan from boiling over.
4. Add freeze dried or dehydrated foods early on in your recipes to allow time for rehydration.
5. Add powdered milk and eggs, cheese and thickeners to recipes last when heating.
6. When melting snow for water, do not let the bottom of the pan go dry or it will scorch (keep packing the snow down to the bottom).
7. Add extra water at high altitudes when boiling (water evaporates more rapidly as you gain altitude) and allow longer cooking times – twenty minutes at 1000m, for example, as against ten minutes at sea level.

Cleaning Up

Soap residue can make you sick. Most seasoned campers, after one experience with "soap sickness of the stomach", recommend using only a scouring pad and water. Boiling water can be used to sterilise and, if you have ignored the above advice, is good for removing the remains of your glued-on pasta or cheese dinners. Soak and then scrub.

Use these recyclable plastic bags to store leftovers and to carry away any litter. Leave the wilderness kitchen clean – and ready for your next feat of mealtime magic!

WATER PURIFICATION
by Julian McIntosh

Polluted water can at best lead to discomfort and mild ill-ness, at worst to death, so the travelling layman needs to know not only what methods and products are available for water purification but also how to improvise a treatment system in an emergency.

Three points about advice on water treatment cause mis-understanding. Firstly, there is no need to kill or remove all the micro-organisms in water. Germs do not necessarily cause disease. Only those responsible for diseases transmitted by drinking water need be treated. And even some water-borne diseases are harmless when drunk. Legionnaires' disease, for example, is caught by breathing in droplets of water containing the bacteria, and not by drinking them.

Secondly, in theory, no normal treatment method will produce infinitely safe drinking water. There is always a chance, however small, that a germ might, by virtue of small size or resistance to chemicals or heat, survive and cause disease. But the more exacting your water treatment process, the smaller the risk – until such time as the risk is so tiny as to be discounted. The skill of the experts lies in assessing when water is, in practice, safe to drink. Unfortunately different experts set their standards at different levels.

Thirdly, beware the use of words like "pure", "disinfect" and "protection", common claims in many manufacturers' carefully written prose. Read the descriptions critically and you will find that most are not offering absolutely safe water but only a relative improvement.

Suspended Solids

If you put dirty water in a glass the suspended solids are the tiny particles that do not readily sink to the bottom. The resolution of the human eye is about one-hundredth of a millimetre, a particle half that size (five microns) is totally invisible to the naked eye and yet there can be over ten million such particles in a litre of water without any visible trace. Suspended solids are usually materials such as decaying vegetable matter or mud and clay. Normally mud and clay contamination is harmless, but extremely fine rock particles including mica or asbestos occasionally remain in glacier water or water running through some types of clay.

Microbiological Contamination

Eggs, worms, flukes, etc.: Organisms, amongst others, that lead to infections of roundworm (*Ascaris*), canine roundworm (*Toxocara canis*), guinea worm (*Dracunculus*) and bilharzia (*Schistosomiasis*). They are relatively large, although still microscopic, and can be removed by even crude forms of filtration. The very tiny black things that you sometimes see wriggling in very still water are insect larvae, not germs, and are not harmful. Practically any form of pre-treatment will remove them.

Protozoa: In this group of small, single-celled animals are the organisms that cause giardiasis (*Giardia lamblia*), an unpleasant form of chronic diarrhoea, and amoebic dysentery (*Entamoeba histolytica*). Both of these protozoa have a cyst stage in their life cycle, during which they are inert and resistant to some forms of chemical treatment. However, they quickly become active and develop when they encounter suitable conditions such as the human digestive tract. They are sufficiently large to be separable from the water by the careful use of some types of pre-filter.

Bacteria: Very small, single-celled organisms responsible for many illnesses from cholera, salmonella, typhoid and bacillary dysentery, to the many less serious forms of diarrhoea known to travellers as Montezuma's Revenge or Delhi Belly. A healthy person would need to drink thousands of a particular bacterium to catch the disease. Luckily, the harmful bacteria transmitted by drinking contaminated water are fairly "soft" and succumb to chemical treatment – their minute size means only a very few filters can be relied upon to remove them all.

Viruses: These exceptionally small organisms live and multiply within host cells. Some viruses such as hepatitis A and a variety of intestinal infections are transmitted through drinking water. Even the finest filters are too coarse to retain viruses. The polio and hepatitis viruses are about 50 times smaller than the pore size in even the finest ceramic filter.

Selection of a Water Supply

Whatever method of water treatment you use, it is essential to start with the best possible supply of water. Learning to assess the potential suitability of a water supply is one of the traveller's most useful skills.

Good points: Ground water, e.g. wells, boreholes, springs. Water away from or upstream of human habitation. Fast running water. Water above a sand or rock bed. Clear, colourless and odourless water.

Bad points: Water close to sources of industrial, human or animal contamination. Stagnant water. Water containing decaying vegetation. Water with odour or a scum on its surface. Discoloured or muddy water.

Wells and boreholes can be contaminated by debris and excreta falling or being washed in from the surface, so the top should be protected. A narrow wall will stop debris. A broad wall is not so effective as people will stand on it and dirt from their feet can fall in. Any wall is better than no wall at all. Fast running water is a hostile environment for the snails that support bilharzia.

Pre-treatment

If you are using water from a river, pool or lake, try to not to draw in extra dirt from the bottom or floating debris from the surface. If the source is surface water such as a lake or river, and very poor, some benefit may even be gained by digging a hole adjacent to the source. As the water seeps through, a form of pre-filtration will take place, leaving behind at least the coarsest contamination.

Pouring the water through finely woven fabrics will also remove some of the larger contamination. If you have fine, clean sand available, perhaps taken from a stream or lake bed, an improvised sand filter can be made using a tin can or similar container with a hole in the bottom. Even a (clean!) sock will do. Pour the water into the top, over the sand. Take care to disturb the surface of the sand as little as possible. Collect the water that has drained through the sand. The longer the filter is used, the better the quality of the water, so re-filter or discard the first water poured through. Discard the contaminated sand after use.

If you are able to store the water without disturbing it, you could also try sedimentation. Much of the dirt in water will settle out if left over a long enough period. Bilharzia flukes die after about 48 hours. The cleaner water can then be drawn off at the top. Very great care will be needed not to disturb the dirt at the bottom. Siphoning is the best method.

If the water you are using has an unpleasant taste or smell, an improvement can be achieved by using coarsely crushed wood charcoal wrapped in cloth. When the "bag" of charcoal is placed in the water or the water is run through the charcoal (like a sand filter) the organic chemicals responsible for practically all the unpleasant tastes and smells will be removed. Some colour improvement may also be noticed. The water will still not be safe to drink without further treatment but you should notice some benefit.

Treatment of a Water Supply

Boiling: Boiling at 100°C kills all the harmful organisms found in water except a few such as slow viruses and spores which are not dangerous if drunk. However, as your altitude above sea level increases, the weight of the atmosphere above you decreases, the air pressure drops, as does the temperature at which water boils. A rule of thumb for calculating this is that water boils at 1°C less for every 300 metres of altitude. Thus if you are on the summit of Kilimanjaro, at 5895 metres, the water will boil at only 80°C.

At temperatures below 100°C, most organisms can still be killed but it takes longer. At temperatures below 70°C, some of the harmful organisms can survive indefinitely and as the temperature continues to drop, so they will flourish.

There is one more important consideration. When water is boiling vigorously there is a lot of turbulence and all the water is at the same temperature. While water is coming to the boil, even if bubbles are rising, there is not only a marked and important difference between the temperature of the water and the temperature at a full boil but there can also be a substantial difference in temperature between water in different parts of the pan, with the result that harmful organisms may still be surviving.

To make water safe for drinking you should bring water to a full boil for at least two minutes. Boil water for one minute extra for every 300 metres above sea level. Do not cool water down with untreated water.

Filtration: The key to understanding the usefulness of a filter is ensuring that you know the size of the particles that the filter will reliably separate, and the dirt load the filter can tolerate before it clogs up. If the pores in the filter are too large, harmful particles can pass through. If small enough to stop harmful particles, the pores can block up quickly, preventing any more water from being filtered.

To reduce this problem, manufacturers employ ingenious means to increase the filter area, and filter in at progressively smaller stages. But even in one apparently clean litre of water there can be a hundred thousand million particles the same size or larger than bacteria. And to stop a bacterium, the filter has to take out all the other particles as well. If the filter is small (of the drinking straw type for instance) or if the water is at all visibly dirty, the filter will block in next to no time.

There are three solutions: water can be filtered first through a coarse filter to remove most of the dirt, and then again through a fine filter to remove the harmful bacteria; a re-cleanable filter can be used; or finally, only apparently clean water could be used with the filter. The use of a coarser filter is called pre-filtration. Viruses are so small they cannot be filtered out of drinking water by normal means. However, because they are normally found with their host infected cells and these are large enough to be filtered, the finest filters are also able to reduce the risk of virus infection from drinking water.

A filter collects quite a lot of miscellaneous debris on its surface and in order to prevent this providing a breeding ground for bacteria, the filter needs to be sterilised from time to time. Some are self-sterilising and need no action but others should be boiled for 20 to 30 minutes at least once every two weeks.

Where filters are described as combining a chemical treatment, this is for self-sterilisation. The chemical is in such small concentrations and in contact with water passing through the filter for such a short period that its use in improving the quality of the filtered water is negligible.

Pre-filtration: Pre-filters should remove particles larger than five to ten microns in size and be very simple to maintain. They will be more resistant to clogging since they take out only the larger particles. They will remove larger microbiological contamination including protozoal cysts, flukes and larger debris that might form a refuge for bacteria and viruses. Pre-filtration is normally adequate for washing. Further treatment is essential for safe drinking supplies.

Fine filtration: To remove all harmful bacteria from water a filter must remove all particles larger than 0.5 microns (some harmless bacteria are as small as 0.2 microns). Filters using a disposable cartridge are generally more compact and have high initial flow rates but are more expensive to operate. Alternatively there are ceramic filters that use porous ceramic "candles". These have low flow rates and are fairly heavy. Some need special care in transport to ensure they do not get cracked or chipped thus enabling untreated water to get through. Ceramic filters can be cleaned easily and are very economic in use.

Activated carbon/charcoal filters: These remove a very wide range of chemicals from water including chlorine and iodine and can greatly improve the quality and palatability of water. But they do not kill or remove germs and may even provide an ideal breeding ground unless self-sterilising. Some filters combine carbon and other elements to improve the taste and this also removes harmful organisms.

Chemical Treatment

There are broadly three germicidal chemicals used for drinking water treatment. For ease of use, efficiency and storage life, the active chemical is usually made up as a tablet suitable for a fixed volume of water, although the heavier the contamination, the larger the dose required.

Germs can also be embedded in other matter and protected from the effects of a chemical, so where water is visibly dirty you must pre-filter first. Chlorine and iodine have no lasting germicidal effect so on no account should untreated water be added to water already treated.

Silver: Completely harmless, taste-free and very long lasting effect, protecting stored water for up to six months. The sterilisation process is quite slow and it is necessary to leave water for at least two hours before use. Silver compounds are not effective against cysts of Amoeba and Giardia, so use pre-filtration first if the water is of poor quality.

Chlorine: Completely harmless, fast-acting and 100 per cent effective if used correctly. A minimum of ten minutes is required before water can be used. The cysts of Amoeba and Giardia are about ten times more resistant to chlorine than bacteria but both are killed if treatment time and dose are adequate. If in doubt, we recommend that the period before use be extended to at least 20 and preferably 30 minutes.

If heavy contamination is suspected, double the dosage. Alternatively, pre-filter. Some people find the taste of chlorine unpleasant particularly if larger doses are being used. The concentration of chlorine drops quickly over several hours and more so in warm temperatures so there is very little lasting effect. Excess chlorine may be removed using Sodium Thiosulphate or carbon filters.

Iodine: Fast acting and very effective, normally taking ten minutes before water is safe to use. It has a quicker action against cysts than chlorine. Double dosage and extended treatment times or pre-filtration are still very strongly recommended if heavy contamination is suspected. Iodine is more volatile than chlorine and the lasting effect is negligible. Excess iodine may be removed by Sodium Thiosulphate or a carbon filter.

Note: Iodine can have serious, lasting physiological side effects and should not be used over an extended period.

Groups particularly at risk are those with thyroid problems and the unborn foetuses of pregnant women. Thyroid problems may only become apparent when the gland is faced with excess iodine, so in the unlikely event of the use of iodine compounds being unavoidable, ask your doctor to arrange for a thyroid test beforehand – or use a good carbon filter to remove excess iodine from the water.

Rules

Order of treatment: If chemical treatment and filtration are being combined, filter first. Filtration removes organic matter which would absorb the chemical and make it less effective. If of a carbon type, the filter will also absorb the chemical leaving none for residual treatment.

In some cases, the filter may also be a source of contamination. If water is being stored prior to treatment then it is worthwhile treating chemically as soon as the water is collected and again after filtration. The first chemical dose prevents algae growing in the stored water.

Storage of water: Use separate containers for treated and untreated water, mark them accordingly and don't mix them up. If you are unable to use separate containers take particular care to sterilise the area round the filler and cap before treated water is stored or at the time treatment takes place. In any case, containers for untreated water should be sterilised every two to three weeks.

Treated water should never be contaminated with any untreated water. Treated water should never be stored in an open container. Treated water left uncovered and not used straight away should be regarded as suspect and re-treated.

COMING HOME
by Col. John Blashford-Snell

Until Rula Lenska joined us on a quest in Nepal I had no idea that actors and expeditioners suffer from the same problem at the end of the show. Both tend to get "post project depression" (PPD) or "after expedition blues".

When a play ends or the filming of a series finishes, Rula explained, the cast is suddenly split up, left to find new jobs or return home for a well-earned rest. The friendships and working relationships break up, the team disappears and a different life style starts overnight. So it is with expeditioners, and, I imagine, ocean voyagers.

Dr John Davies, one of Britain's leading exploration medics, once started a lecture at the Scientific Exploration Society with the statement, "Expeditions may endanger your health". He went on to point out that for the novice, the experience can be an introduction to negative aspects of one's personality easily suppressed in normal daily life. However, with appropriate counselling and support, this can be a journey of self-discovery leading to increased confidence and a more enlightened attitude to others.

Seasoned adventurers, like experienced actors, recognise post expedition blues, the symptoms of which are similar to bereavement. This is triggered by the loss of one's new found "family" of expedition friends in a widely different culture and by suddenly being cut off from the excitement on return home.

"I just can't face going back to nine to five in the Tax office", groaned an Inland Revenue Officer who had spent three months in the Gobi. Routine and mundane lifestyle aggravate the condition and for many it is cured only by involvement in another challenge. Returning travellers also face isolation from family and colleagues, who have no concept of their recent intense experience. They are often perplexed by the indifferent response to their stories and may end up silent and withdrawn. The envy and resentment of the uninitiated, who imagine that one has been on a jolly picnic or at best some self-inflicted masochism, is also common.

"Don't know what you've done to my mother", complained a son after his mum had returned from one of the Discovery Expeditions in South America, "She's awfully quiet". But meeting the lady in question at a reunion a few months later, I found her in great spirits, reliving the experience with her old pals.

John Davies, with whom I have been on many trips, advises "returnees", especially the older ones, to spend several days enquiring about the day to day problems that have occurred in their absence, before slowly beginning to recount their experiences. So, on being met by my wife as I stepped off a comfortable British Airways flight from Delhi recently, I asked, "How are those new trees in the garden coming on?" "Have you gone mad?" replied Judith, well used to a dozen tales of high adventure before we reached the car park. But perhaps I'm beyond hope!

However, there may be medical problems, as I discovered a year after a Sandhurst expedition in Ethiopia when my right leg started shaking uncontrollably whilst I was lecturing. "How strange", I thought, trying not to notice the offending limb. Two weeks later, lying racked with a fever in hospital, it was found that I had malaria, by which time I also had blurred vision and had lost twenty pounds in weight. But once diagnosed, malaria is usually fairly easily cured and the doctors knew I'd been to the tropics.

Sadly not all ailments are so quickly dealt with, as I realised after twelve months of visits to the St. Pancras Hospital for Tropical Diseases. Strange hot flushes, violent stabbing pains in my stomach, aches and itches in awkward places were making life extremely uncomfortable. "There's

nothing wrong with you," boomed one of the world's leading specialists in tropical diseases, after exhaustive tests
proved negative. "You young fellows imagine you've
caught everything under the sun if you spend six weeks in
the jungle. When I was in Burma ..." he droned on. My
morale was at rock bottom and it took great courage to
return to the hospital a few weeks later, after the symptoms
had become almost unbearable.

As luck would have it, a charming and much more sym-
pathetic Asian doctor was on duty and in no time he had me
face down on a trolley with a flexible viewing device inserted up my rear end and my shirt over my head. "Keep him
still," he beseeched as two strapping Fijian nurses pinned
me down. "Oh! my goodness," exclaimed the physician.
"What a fine example. Excuse me, sir, but you have a splen-
did parasite. It is quite unusual to see one so well developed.
Would you mind if we allowed a class of medical students
to see it?" Before I could even protest, I was wheeled in to
a theatre full of students, many of them, I noted, looking
between my legs, were extremely attractive young women.
One by one they came forward, without even a titter, to peer
intently up my bottom. At last I was taken away and the
awful tube removed. "What now?" I asked. "Oh – just swal-
low these pills and you'll be as right as rain" smiled the doctor.

So it is my advice that if you feel ill after an overseas visit,
go straight to your GP and say where you have been. Mark
you, they might diagnose jet lag, which can affect one more
than most care to admit.

This book contains useful tips on surviving the onslaught
and reducing the effects of jet lag to the minimum so I'll not
dwell on it. Suffice to say that when I get home I keep going
until nightfall, doing simple uncomplicated things like
unpacking or weeding, then I take a very mild sleeping pill
and totter off to bed. With luck I can usually sleep for six

hours. The important thing is to avoid stressful situations and not to make any important decisions until after your body has readjusted. In my case this is usually 24 hours. Indeed, even weeding may not be a good idea. Having stepped off a long flight from Mongolia, I pulled up all my wife's carefully planted ground cover instead of the weeds.

If I am still feeling low, I concentrate on writing my thank-you letters (if not done on the 'plane!) and amending my packing list, whilst memory of all the things I forgot to take and all unnecessary items that went with me is still fresh. Then it's down to sorting out photos, slides, videos and writing reports and articles. Next comes repairs to kit, getting cameras serviced and preparing lectures.

If you start to feel sorry for yourself, you are not really bringing the benefits of your experiences to your life at home. Indeed I expect you will find that you have changed but the world has not.

The whole point is to keep active and look forward to the next challenge, and, if you can't afford another trip, why not use your vigour and energy to help others in your area, sick children, old people or anyone who could use some voluntary assistance.

The great cry is, if you want to avoid PPD, keep busy.

Chapter Four
TRAVELLERS' DISEASES

TRAVELLERS' DISEASES

In reading this chapter, one might be forgiven for thinking that going abroad is the quickest way of signing your life away, or your admission form for the nearest available hospital, as you are certain to pick up some exotic disease or another. So far we have dealt with the prevention of disease and those niggling everyday health concerns. Here, however, we tackle the big problems, the diseases that keep you awake at night in a cold sweat at the mere thought of contracting them.

The aim here, though, is to allay your fears by equipping you with the knowledge to deal with these problems in the unlikely event that they do actually arise. Though the chances of you having diarrhoeal symptoms may be as much as 50 per cent, the chances of you catching malaria whilst abroad are between two and three per cent (see percentage risk chart on p. 203).

The chapter begins with essays on some of the most feared diseases of the moment and some of the problems you are most likely to encounter, such as dealing with the heat, to give you a more balanced idea of what to expect and how to combat the problems if you do contract them. This is then followed by a list of other equally unpleasant diseases; their symptoms, so that you will have more of a clue as to what it is you are ailing from; and the cures available. So let us begin with the bane of all tropical travellers: malaria.

MALARIA

by Drs Sharon Welby and Nick Beeching

Malaria remains rife throughout much of the tropics, and causes a huge burden in terms of illness and death for the indigenous population. It poses a significant and difficult problem for the traveller. The ever-changing pattern of drug resistance, along with concerns about the side-effects of anti-malarial drugs, has resulted in confusion regarding selection of treatment. Awareness of the very real hazard of malaria and the importance of gaining accurate pre-travel advice is vital for travellers to the tropics.

Malaria is a parasitic blood infection transmitted by the bite of the female anopheline mosquito. There are four types of malaria: *Plasmodium falciparum*, *Plasmodium ovale*, *Plasmodium vivax* and *Plasmodium malariae*. *P. falciparum*, also known as malignant malaria, is the most serious: more than two million people living in endemic areas die as a result of it each year. In spite of persisting efforts, adequate control of malaria has not yet been achieved and there is a significant risk for travellers to most parts of the Indian Sub-continent and the Far East, sub-Saharan Africa and parts of Central and South America. The risks in North Africa and countries in the east Mediterranean littoral and the Middle East are more variable.

The Illness

The incubation period after a mosquito bite varies from a minimum of eight to ten days up to several years. Most people who are infected by falciparum malaria develop symptoms within a couple of months, but the longest symptom-free period we have seen was over a year. The earliest symptoms are non-specific and are often wrongly diagnosed as 'flu or gastroenteritis. Most people develop symptoms of fever, headache and generalised aches and pains, and about a quarter of people suffer pronounced vomiting and diarrhoea. It is therefore essential that travellers have an immediate blood test for malaria if they develop a fever a week after arriving in a malarious area or within a year of their return. If left untreated, patients (especially expatriates who have not been exposed to malaria before) can rapidly develop high fevers or lapse into a coma and die. Between five and 15 people die of malaria infection in the UK each year, and many of these are due to delay in seeking medical advice.

The other three forms of malaria are rarely life-threatening but can have a more prolonged incubation period of up to two years. They cannot be distinguished from life-threatening falciparum malaria unless a blood film is examined. These three forms of malaria sometimes recur after effective treatment of the first illness, so further drug treatment is usually required with a drug called primaquine.

Prevention

Personal protection for the traveller focuses on two main aspects: the first is to prevent being bitten by mosquitoes; and the second relies on taking antimalarial drugs regularly. When a malaria-carrying mosquito bites a person, the malaria parasites travel to the liver via the blood stream and develop there without causing any signs of illness. Once the parasite is ready, it leaves the liver and attacks the red blood cells. This is the stage at which anti-malarial drugs act, by preventing the parasite from infecting blood cells and thereby preventing the symptoms of malaria from developing. It is important to keep taking anti-malarials regularly while abroad, so that drug levels in the blood are sufficient to prevent disease, and to continue taking the drugs for four weeks after leaving the malarious area so that the incubation period after any potential bites is covered by the drugs.

The malaria-carrying mosquitoes bite from dusk to dawn

and bites can be prevented by using a combination of methods:

• Wearing shirts and trousers after dusk. Clothing can also be soaked in repellent: 30 millilitres of repellent dissolved in 250 millilitres of water is an effective mixture.

• Sleeping in an air-conditioned or a screened room, or under a bed net, preferably one impregnated with permethrin (0.2 grams of permethrin per metre of material).

• Repelling and killing any mosquitoes which have entered the bedroom with pyrethrum sprays, mosquito coils or electrical insecticide dispensers. Electronic buzzers are not effective.

• Using repellents containing diethyltoluamide (DEET) or using the new eucalyptus-based repellent *Mosiguard Natural*.

Anti-malarial Drugs

Anti-malarial drug therapy is an area fraught with difficulty. The changing pattern of drug resistance, together with possible side-effects of the drugs, have made it increasingly difficult to choose the correct regimens. With this in mind it is advisable for all travellers to obtain specialist advice prior to their trip. In Britain there are currently four main anti-malarial drugs in use: chloroquine, proguanil, mefloquine and doxycycline.

Chloroquine and Proguanil

Chloroquine and proguanil (*Paludrine*) are the oldest and most widely used. They are safe to take long-term (however, eye check-ups are recommended after three years of use) and the wealth of experience suggests that they are safe to use during pregnancy. Unfortunately, there is now widespread resistance to these drugs rendering them much less effective in some parts of the world. Depending on the area to be visited, they are either taken alone or together. Travellers should start anti-malarials at least a week before travel, mainly to make sure that they do not react to the medication, continue whilst there and for at least four weeks after leaving a malarious area. The usual adult dose is chloroquine two tablets once a week together with proguanil two tablets daily (a total of 16 tablets per week). The main side-effects of the chloroquine/proguanil combination (apart from an unpleasant taste) are nausea, stomach upsets and mouth ulcers. Chloroquine should not be taken by people who are currently suffering from epilepsy or have had epilepsy in the past, or by people who suffer from psoriasis, a common skin disorder.

Mefloquine (*Lariam*)

There has been a lot of controversy surrounding the use of mefloquine for malaria prophylaxis. Publicity in the media and conflicting medical advice have led to confusion, and subsequently some travellers are not taking any drug prophylaxis at all for countries where it is recommended. This could lead to potentially life-threatening malaria infection. Every traveller needs to consider the pros and cons of mefloquine and decide if the drug is suitable for them.

Mefloquine is first choice for areas where there is widespread chloroquine resistance such as sub-Saharan Africa, the Amazonian basin and parts of South East Asia. Mefloquine is not suitable for everyone and it should not be taken by:

• women in the first 12 weeks of pregnancy, women who are breast-feeding or women who might become pregnant within three months of taking the last tablet.

• people with a history of epilepsy or a strong family history of epilepsy.

- people who have any mental health problems, e.g. depression, anxiety attacks or mood disturbances.

- people who are taking certain kinds of blood pressure tablets (ß blockers).

- people whose jobs depend on a high degree of co-ordination, such as airline pilots or professional divers.

- young children under 15 kilograms (this limit may be lowered soon).

- people with severe kidney or liver problems.

Studies from Africa show that mefloquine is more effective at preventing malaria infection then a combination of chloroquine and proguanil (90 per cent compared to 60-70 per cent). Mefloquine is also convenient to take as it is a weekly dose and it is now licensed to be used for up to one year. However, it is relatively expensive.

All drugs have side effects: studies have shown that mefloquine can cause problems such as dizziness, headaches, insomnia, vivid dreams and depression in a few people. A recent study showed that around a quarter of those people taking mefloquine and an eighth taking chloroquine and proguanil experienced these problems. Some studies have shown that in about one in ten people the side-effects interfered with planned activities, and that in one in 10,000 people a severe side-effect occurred. The majority of side-effects with mefloquine begin within three weeks of starting the drug and stop within three weeks of stopping. It is recommended that you start mefloquine at least two weeks before travelling so that if any side-effects should occur you can change to an alternative drug.

Doxycycline

The third alternative is an antibiotic called doxycycline (a form of tetracycline). This is particularly popular with

Australian travellers but British authorities mainly recommend it for travellers to the border areas of Thailand/Myanmar (Burma) and Thailand/Cambodia as well as the western province of Cambodia, where *falciparum* malaria is often resistant to both chloroquine and mefloquine. Doxycycline should not be taken by pregnant women or children under the age of eight. It should be taken with liberal quantities of fluid to prevent ulceration and discomfort in the œsophagus. The main side-effect is that some people become very sensitive to the sun and become sunburnt easily (a good sun tan cream is recommended – factor 15+). Doxycycline interferes with the contraceptive pill and it is recommended that women also use barrier methods of contraception in the first two weeks of starting doxycycline. Women taking regular doxycycline may be prone to recurrent vaginal thrush. Balancing these side effects, doxycycline provides good anti-malarial protection and also reduces the incidence and duration of travellers' diarrhoea.

New Guidelines

The new British guidelines balance the risk of malaria infection with the possible side effects of antimalarial drugs. The guidelines continue to support the use of mefloquine by people who have no contraindications to the drug and who are visiting regions where the risk of malaria is high. However, the guidelines state that an alternative to mefloquine for people on package tours of two weeks or less to the east African coast (and who are not planning to stay in rural areas or go on safari) is the less protective chloroquine and proguanil regimen. This minimises the risk of side effects but the need to take precautions against mosquito bites is even greater. The guidelines for the Gambia suggest that chloroquine and proguanil will give reasonable protection from January to May whereas mefloquine is the drug of choice for the rest of the year.

Children and Pregnant Women

Children require lower doses of anti-malarials, depending on their age and weight. They soon learn to dislike both chloroquine and proguanil. Although chloroquine syrup is available, proguanil is only available as tablets. The tablets can be ground up and hidden in treats (jam, sandwiches, chocolates etc.) to persuade children to take them. Pregnant women are prone to severe malaria attacks and should be advised not to travel to areas with a significant malaria risk – especially sub-Saharan Africa – unless it is unavoidable, when they must take malaria prophylaxis. It is recommended that pregnant women also take folic acid (a vitamin) at the same time as proguanil.

Expatriates

Long-term expatriates are more difficult to advise. Many adopt a "macho" attitude to malaria and discontinue any malaria prophylaxis in the mistaken belief that they have developed protective immunity. Due to the rapid emergence of drug-resistant malaria, we believe that this is an unwise option. The best advice will be given on a personal level by your GP because all these cases will be different.

Standby Treatment

The more adventurous traveller going to places where rapid access to medical advice is not available may wish to carry a course of anti-malarial "standby" treatment. This should be taken if symptoms of possible malaria develop, but it is not a substitute for medical care, and it is important to seek medical advice and a blood film. The standby regime will depend on the drug resistance in the area which you are visiting and on which anti-malarial drugs are being taken. It is advisable to seek specialist advice. Some examples of standby medications are:

Fansidar – three tablets taken at the same time is the most convenient, but this is not suitable for people who are allergic to sulpha drugs.

Mefloquine – two tablets taken together followed by two tablets 12 hours later. The main problem with this dose of mefloquine is severe nausea and vomiting and the increased risk of neuropsychiatric side-effects.

Halofantrine – Until recently a third option, halofantrine (*Halfan*) was very popular for self treatment, particularly in East Africa, but side-effects of this drug affecting the heart have now been identified and we recommend that it should not be used.

Quinine – (adult dose two tablets three times a day for three days) and tetracycline (adult dose one tablet four times a day for seven days) are recommended as standby medication in areas with a lot of drug resistance.

Summary

The risk of malaria infection poses a real and significant problem for the traveller. It is essential that pre-travel advice is sought and that each traveller takes anti-mosquito bite measures and decides which anti-malarial drug regime is suitable for them. It is important to remember that no anti-malarial drug is 100 per cent effective and any illness, especially if there is fever, must lead to a blood test to exclude malaria infection. It is also important to inform the doctor that you have been to a malarious area within the preceding two years. If this advice is ignored, the diagnosis of malaria will not be considered until too late, and tragic and preventable deaths will continue to occur.

TRAVELLERS' DISEASES

Key Points

1. Take measures to prevent mosquito bites:

repellents
impregnated bed nets
suitable clothing
sleep in a screened room and use knock down
insecticides, coils or electronic vapourisers.

2. Take appropriate anti-malarial drugs regularly and complete the course.

3. Remember that no prophylaxis is 100 per cent effective and in the event of any illness, especially if there is fever, seek immediate diagnosis (with a blood film) and treatment.

4. Consider carrying "standby treatment".

DIARRHOEAL ILLNESS
by Dr Nick Beeching

The world-wide distribution of travellers' diarrhoea is reflected in its many geographical synonyms – Delhi Belly, the Aztec two-step, Turista, Malta dog, Rangoon runs, to name but a few. Typically, the illness starts a few days after arrival at your destination and consists of diarrhoea without blood, nausea with some vomiting and perhaps a mild fever. The mainstay of treatment is adequate rehydration and rest, and the illness is usually self-limiting within a few days. Antibiotics to treat or prevent this common illness are not usually prescribed in anticipation of an infection. Exceptions to this rule are business travellers or others embarking on short trips (less than two to three weeks) for whom even a short period of illness would be disastrous, e.g. athletes attending international meetings.

The most important aspect for the treatment of diarrhoea is the replacement of fluids and salts that have been lost from the body. For most adults, non-carbonated, non-alcoholic drinks that do not contain large amounts of sugar are quite adequate. For adults with prolonged diarrhoea, and for children, it is more important to use balanced weak salt solutions which contain a small amount of sugar that promotes absorption of the salts. These can be obtained in pre-packaged sachets of powder (e.g. *Dioralyte, Rehidrat*) that are convenient to carry and are dissolved in a fixed amount of sterile water. *Dioralyte* can also be bought in the UK as effervescent tablets.

If pre-packaged mixtures are not available, a simple rehydration solution can be prepared by adding eight level teaspoonfuls of sugar or honey and half a teaspoon of salt to one litre of water (with flavouring to tempt small children).

Nausea, which frequently accompanies diarrhoea, can usually be overcome by taking small amounts of fluid as often as possible. For small children it may be necessary to give spoonfuls of fluid every few minutes for prolonged periods. If you or your child have severe vomiting which prevents any fluids being taken, medical attention must be sought immediately.

Anti-diarrhoeal drugs are not usually recommended and should rarely be given to children. Kaopectate is safe for children aged over two years but not very effective (kaolin and morphine should not be carried). For adults, codeine phosphate, loperamide (*Imodium* or *Arret*) or diphenoxylate (*Lomotil*) are sometimes useful. These drugs should never be given to children and should not be used for bloody or prolonged diarrhoea. They are best reserved for occasional use to prevent accidents while travelling – for example before a prolonged rural bus trip. Prolonged use of these medications may prevent your body from eliminating the diarrhoea – encouraging organisms and toxins – and may also lead to constipation.

Preparations containing clioquinol are still widely available outside the UK, where it was previously sold under the trade name *Enterovioform*. These preparations are useless and should not be taken (they have been linked with severe side effects in some parts of the world). Other than rehydration solutions or the medications discussed in this section, I do not recommend purchasing medicines for diarrhoea from pharmacies or chemists.

Prevention

Travellers who wish to prevent diarrhoea should consult their doctor about preventative medication (a controversial issue within the profession) before travel. Liquid bismuth preparations (not an antibiotic) are effective but huge volumes need to be carried in luggage (very messy if broken) and bismuth tablets are difficult to obtain in the UK. Various groups of antibiotics may be used, including tetracyclines (e.g. doxycycline), sulphur containing antibiotics (e.g. *Steptrotriad* or cotrimoxazole, *Septrin* or *Bactrim*) and quinolone agents (e.g. ciprofloxacin, norfloxacin).

Prophylactic antibiotics are not recommended for the majority of travellers because of the limited duration of effectiveness and the possibility of side effects, including, paradoxically, diarrhoea.

Self-treatment

Self-treatment with antibiotics for established diarrhoeal illness is usually inappropriate unless qualified medical attention is impossible to obtain. Travellers to remote areas may wish to carry a course of antibiotics for this eventuality. Bloody diarrhoea with abdominal pain and fever may be due to bacillary dysentery (shigella organisms) or a variety of other organisms such as campylobacter or salmonella. The most appropriate antibiotic would be a quinolone such as ciprofloxacin, or a sulphur drug such as cotrimoxazole. Prolonged bloody diarrhoea with mucus (jelly), especially without much fever, may be due to amoebic dysentery, which can be treated with metronidazole (*Flagyl*) or tinidazole (*Fasigyn*).

Prolonged, explosive diarrhoea with pale creamy motions may be due to giardia, a common hazard for overlanders travelling through the Indian subcontinent. This responds to metronidazole or tinidazole. These two antibiotics should not be taken at the same time as alcohol because of severe reactions between them.

If you have to treat yourself, obtain qualified medical investigation and help at the earliest opportunity. This is essential if symptoms do not settle after medication. Travellers who anticipate the need for self-treatment should take Dr Richard Dawood's book *Travellers' Health: How to Stay Healthy Abroad* (OUP). Diarrhoea may be caused by other, more severe illnesses, including typhoid and malaria, and these will need specific treatment.

HIV/AIDS AND SEX ABROAD
by Drs Nick Beeching and Sharon Welby

HIV infection resulting from sex abroad is the single most frequent cause of lethal infection in travellers. In 1996 about 80 per cent of all heterosexually acquired HIV in the UK was acquired as a result of sex overseas. 85 per cent originated in Africa but in other regions the risk is increasing. This is possibly just the tip of the iceberg as many HIV infections go undiagnosed in the UK because travellers do not realise the increased dangers of having sex with a new partner in a high HIV prevalence country and therefore do not present themselves for HIV screening.

The commonest route for the spread of HIV infection world-wide is through heterosexual intercourse, despite the emphasis in the western press on "high risk groups" such as homosexual men and intravenous drug users. The HIV/AIDS epidemic is rampant in Africa, which has 90 per cent of the reported HIV/AIDS cases, and in some areas of the world up to 90 per cent of the "pay for sex workers" of both sexes are HIV positive and as many as one in three of the adult population are infected. HIV rates are rapidly increasing in India, countries around the "Golden Triangle" and many other parts of the tropics and former USSR. The risk of becoming infected with HIV from a single sexual encounter is 0.1-1 per cent and is passed on more frequently from male to female. This risk is also increased in the presence of ulcerative genital disease.

The risk of HIV infection may be reduced by using condoms, especially condoms with spermicide. Buy condoms before travelling (look for the British standards kitemark) and use them. A Swedish study of nearly 1000 women showed that 28 per cent had had casual travel sex, more than 85 per cent of their partners had originated from Europe, 76 per cent of them were drunk during casual sex and only nine per cent used a condom. In Britain an anonymous study of travellers attending the Hospital for Tropical Diseases for tropical disease screening found that the HIV rate in heterosexual men was 1.2 per cent.

In reality it is not possible to construct a world map showing global distribution of risk, as a lot of under-reporting goes on for a variety of social, cultural and economic reasons. An article in *The Guardian* in November 1997 reported that whilst the Mongolian government maintains that there is only one HIV-positive male in the country, the WHO states that "the STD infection rate indicates there are currently around 100 HIV-positive Mongolians". While some places certainly have a higher incidence of sexually-transmitted diseases than others, it is important to bear in mind that the risk depends on behaviour as well as geography – easy sex is the greatest risk factor.

HIV eventually causes AIDS in the majority of people who have been infected. The interval between infection and the development of AIDS, however, may be more than ten years. At present there is no vaccine against HIV infection and there is no treatment, although medical management of HIV positive individuals is improving dramatically. The majority of HIV positive individuals are unaware that they have been infected and cannot be distinguished from non-infected people. HIV is not transmitted by hugging or social kissing, or using the same toilet seat, swimming pool or cup as a HIV infected person. There is no evidence that it is transmitted by mosquitoes or other insects.

Hepatitis B

Hepatitis B is another virus infection that is widespread in the tropics and local people are usually infected before birth or in early childhood. A minority will continue to carry the virus but will have no obvious signs of infection. This minority is large – up to 20 per cent of young adults in the Far East and five to 15 per cent of young adults in Africa, the Middle East and South and Central America. Hepatitis B is spread by the same means as HIV but is 100 times more infectious than HIV and may also be spread by bed bugs. There is an effective vaccine available for hepatitis B, (see *Vaccines* p. 27 in Chapter One).

Other Sexually Transmitted Diseases (STDs)

It has been estimated that each year one in 20 adolescents world-wide contracts a sexually transmitted disease. The most serious ones are HIV and hepatitis B but the classical venereal diseases such as syphilis and gonorrhoea are extremely common. The incidence of syphilis has been increasing in the former states of the USSR, and some of the eastern European countries have taken over from the more traditional "sex tourism" countries. There is world-wide concern about the spread of multiresistant gonorrhoea which means that if this disease is acquired abroad it may be harder to treat. A new sexual encounter anywhere in the world can pass on the usual infections such as lice, NSU (non-specific urethritis), herpes and genital warts but travel to the tropics can lead to an occasional exotic infection such as chancroid which causes a genital ulcerative condition.

Self-medication should not be attempted and any sexual encounter with a new partner while travelling should be followed by a detailed check up on return home even if no symptoms are apparent. The Swedish study showed that one in four of the women who considered themselves healthy had a current STD or a vaginal condition called bacterial vaginosis on screening.

BILHARZIA (SCHISTOSOMIASIS)
by Drs Sharon Welby and Nick Beeching

In many areas of Africa, the Middle East and some parts of South America and the Far East, the fresh water lakes and rivers are infested with a parasite which causes schistosomiasis (commonly known as bilharzia). The World Health Organisation estimates that at present 200 million people are infected with schistosomiasis in 76 countries in the tropics and sub tropics.

You may become infected with this parasite if you wade or swim through fresh water lakes, rivers, ponds, reservoirs, dams, irrigation ditches or even temporary bodies of water, in endemic areas. Even deep water far off a lake shore cannot be regarded as safe from schistosomiasis. Swimming pools and showers which are supplied by untreated stream water can also be a source of infection. However, if the swimming pool is adequately treated with chlorine it is usually safe and any water which is left to stand for three days is safe (as long as it is stored in a snail-free environment) because the infective larvae form only survives for 48 hours in water. Neglected swimming pools and dams can become rapidly colonised with snails (which are involved in the schistosome life-cycle) which would make them unsafe for swimming in. Human schistosomiasis cannot be acquired by swimming and wading in salt water. Travellers are commonly misinformed by the locals (and tour operators) about the presence of schistosomiasis in lakes or rivers and, since there is no practical way to distinguish infested from non-infested water and no protective vaccine is available, fresh water swimming in endemic areas should be avoided. Watersports are particularly dangerous because they may involve exposure over a large area of surface water.

Life Cycle

Infected snails release large numbers of minute free-swim-ming larvae (called *cercariae*) into the water. When humans come in contact with infested fresh water the cercariae are capable of penetrating the unbroken skin. After penetration the larva spends a period of time travelling around the body before it develops into an adult blood fluke. The adult then finds a partner and settles down in the blood vessels around the bladder or around the liver (depending on the species) to produce eggs at the rate of 300-1500 per day. These eggs then pass out in the urine or faeces to the outside world and find their way into water, where they hatch to produce the larvae form that infects a snail and so the cycle continues. The time from the cercariae penetrating the skin to the adults producing eggs is usually four to 12 weeks. The flukes do not multiply within humans so the number of flukes is related to the initial exposure and, in general, severe illness only occurs after a heavy exposure over a long period of time.

The Symptoms

Usually there are no symptoms with schistosomiasis infection but occasionally people notice a generalised weakness and feeling of ill health. There may be an initial tingling of the skin, an itch or occasionally a rash, a few hours after contact with infested water but this is usually short-lived and is due to the larvae penetrating the skin. Sometimes people notice a few chest symptoms (wheezing) three to ten days after infection but this is self-limiting. The eggs of the flukes are detected on laboratory screening of the urine or faeces and there is also a blood test that looks for antibodies (which are protective proteins that fight against the parasite).

A few people develop an acute allergic response to the eggs which usually occurs about two to three weeks or more after infection. This consists of fever, lack of appetite, weight loss, headaches, generalised aches and pains, diarrhoea, cough with or without wheezing and sometimes an itchy rash like "hives". An increased number of white blood cells (called eosinophils) in blood tests give a clue that invasive worms are around. This illness is called "Katayama fever". Once the infection becomes established, abdominal pain and blood in the urine and/or stool can occur. Men sometimes notice change in colour or consistency of their semen. The harmful effects are due to the eggs: they cause bleeding, ulceration, and the formation of small growths as they penetrate the wall of the intestine and bladder. Long-term effects include severe liver damage due to fibrosis, kidney failure and bladder cancer. On very rare occasions, especially with heavy infections, the eggs can find their way to different parts of the body and cause pressure effects. This can result in neurological problems such as weakness in the legs or convulsions.

Prevention and Treatment

If contact with fresh water is unavoidable, try to cross upstream of any villages, cover exposed skin and wear boots. Rubber boots and wetsuits are protective but they must be dried quickly in the sun after use. The larvae die quickly when removed from water and cannot survive drying, so vigorous rubbing with a towel after possible exposure may reduce the chance of infection. If you have had possible exposure to schistosomiasis ask your doctor for schistosomiasis screening tests three months after your last contact with freshwater. There is an effective treatment available which is a single dose of a drug called praziquantel. This is usually well tolerated with only occasional gastro-intestinal side effects.

RABIES
by Jack Barker

A dog staggers down the road, stumbling and growling, foaming at the mouth. Frozen with fear you stay still, hoping it won't see you. Its head swings round, and you look into its bloodshot eyes. It lurches towards you. You scramble on a chair, on a table, but it just keeps coming.

And then you wake up. In the UK there is no rabies – for now – so scenes such as that are purely for nightmares. On the continent the situation is better since the strategic dropping of bait laced with genetically-engineered vaccine, but in many areas of the third world it can be a different matter. Since 1975, 7,000 people in the UK have been treated for suspect bites. Between 1969 and 1989 there were 12 imported cases of human hydrophobia in people who have not sought treatment in time. All were fatal.

For a start, it's not just mad dogs that can transmit the disease. Insect-eating bats, cats and any other mammal can pass it on. Even wild animals pose a risk, made worse by the fact that one of the early symptoms of the illness, before full-blown hydrophobia sets in, can be an uncharacteristic docility. Beware of the rat who comes up to beg for sandwiches!

A headache is an early symptom, but things get worse quickly after that. Fever and spreading paralysis degenerate into episodes of confusion, aggression and hallucination, and by the time the illness has progressed to this stage it is too late for treatment.

The distinctive feature that gives the disease its name is the fear of water – hydrophobia. Attempts to drink produce powerful contractions of the muscles of the neck and those involved in swallowing and breathing, associated with an indescribable terror that would be more appropriate to a horror film. The patient dies after a few days of horrific delirium.

In India alone there are 50,000 deaths from rabies every year. So far only one person who started to display symptoms before being treated has lived to tell the tale. The disease is widespread in parts of South America, the Indian subcontinent, Thailand, and the Philippines. Only a few countries are thought to be completely free of rabies: currently these are; Britain, Ireland, Norway, Sweden, Iceland, Malaysia, New Guinea, Borneo, Taiwan, Japan, Antarctica, Australia, and New Zealand.

Humans can catch rabies from any infected animal, whether domestic or wild, but the most common cause of infection is a bite from a dog. British statistics compiled in 1975 found that 74 per cent of bites reported in returning travellers were inflicted by dogs, 16 per cent by cats, and 12 per cent by wild animals. Surprisingly, the remaining eight per cent were inflicted by monkeys or chimpanzees, which were at the time popular as photo props in Spain. In areas where the disease has become established it tends to circulate within a few specific species. In America, for example, vaccination programmes have largely eliminated canine rabies, but a bite from a North American skunk would present a very real threat of infection. Indian monkeys, African jackals, Central American vampires, insectivorous bats in Europe or the States, Arctic foxes, Indian rats and domestic cats are all quite capable of infecting humans.

Transmission occurs when the infected animal's saliva penetrates the victim's skin through a bite or scratch. However, infection can sometimes take place without broken skin: the virus can get through the membranes in the eye as well as those in the mouth or nose, which explains why the habit some dogs have of licking people's faces is even less popular abroad than it is in the UK. Cases have even occurred where infection has taken place as a result of inhaling the virus – from bat-infested caves or in laboratory accidents – with fatal results.

The incubation period for rabies is usually two to three months, but symptoms can start within a few days, or have been known to lie dormant for several years. Once symptoms show it is too late for treatment.

The virus quickly enters the nerve endings in the muscles and spreads along the nerves to the brain and spinal cord. It is easiest to catch and kill at the site of infection to prevent it reaching this stage. Any animal bite or lick should be cleaned immediately and thoroughly. This should be practised even if there is no risk of rabies, as all animal teeth and saliva are contaminated with a variety of bacteria, viruses, and fungi which are potentially hazardous. The wound should be washed with soap and water, cleaned of broken teeth and debris, and rinsed in liberal amounts of water, (the government advises scrubbing a wound for five minutes under a running tap) and then applying a dilute iodine solution, or alcohol. Gin or whisky will do in an emergency although stronger drink will work better. Mercurochrome, hydrogen peroxide, and the brightly-coloured ammonium antiseptics are not recommended, as they are not good at killing viruses. Deep or dirty wounds should be treated with a broad-spectrum antibiotic, and an injection against tetanus should be considered.

Treatment

The treatment for rabies is not simple, and it is essential to use a doctor who is fully conversant with the procedures. Although alternative medicine can be useful for some illnesses, there are no "alternative" treatments for rabies that have yet been proved to be effective, so do not use herbalists, acupuncturists, gurus, or aromatherapists. Go immediately to a qualified western-trained doctor at the nearest major health facility. There is no recommended minimum for the time that should elapse between possible exposure and the beginning of treatment: all authorities agree that treatment should be started as soon as possible. This is still necessary even if the victim has had a preventative immunisation against the disease. Be suspicious if only offered a simple treatment: no-one should allow themselves to be sent away "cured" after just one injection or tablet. It takes more than that to protect against rabies. There have been cases where bite victims have been charged handsomely for a single injection, sent away "cured", and have died later. UK doctors are recommended to give an immediate injection to boost the immune system, as well as a dose of human diploid cell vaccine. Booster injections should then be given three, seven, 14, 30, and 90 days later.

In the first rush of panic, don't lose your common sense: it would be unwise to accept an injection with a dirty needle from some bush-clinic in Zaïre, or to put much faith in a vaccine that has been stored in the hot tropical sun rather than the refrigerated conditions recommended by the manufacturer. In some parts of the world, the only vaccine on offer might be the old-fashioned painful stomach-injected type. In this situation, it is generally better to organise transportation to somewhere with better medical facilities, even if this means going all the way home.

Because the treatment can be drawn out and expensive, it is well worth keeping track of the animal that inflicted the bite if this is possible. If it stays healthy for ten days, the doctor may decide that it is safe to stop the post-exposure vaccination course.

The new diploid vaccine makes immunisation prior to possible exposure to rabies acceptable for the first time. The old treatment for the illness, though effective, was so unpleasant that it would only be used when absolutely necessary. It involved such a weak vaccine that it needed to be injected in large quantities straight into the stomach. The new diploid vaccine is more effective, but also more expensive: most commercial clinics only administer a tiny dose as a prophylactic. This was never intended to offer more than a partial protection. Although pre-immunisation is thought to extend the length of time that can be allowed to elapse between infection and proper medical treatment, by how much is still unknown. The medical advice is still to see a doctor without delay, so pre-vaccination is only really appropriate for those who will be travelling well off the beaten trail, or handling wild animals. (See also *Vaccines* p. 29 in Chapter One.)

HIGH ALTITUDE, COLD FEET?

by Dr Saye Khoo

The world's high places, long beloved by mountaineers, are increasingly visited by other travellers. The rewards may be great but the risks increase with isolation, likelihood of accidents and altitude-related sickness. The risk of altitude sickness can be minimised with advance preparation, preventative medicine and early treatment so it is vitally important for any prospective trekker to be aware of the possible effects of altitude, to recognise the symptoms and to know how best to combat it when the need arises.

Altitude-related illness rarely occurs below 2500 metres (8200 feet) but becomes more frequent after 3000 metres (9850 feet), the risk increasing with higher ascent. The main areas of the world where this is likely to happen are: the Himalayas (India, Nepal); Karakorams (Pakistan, China); Tibet; the Andes (Chile, Peru, Ecuador, Columbia); Mts. Kenya and Kilimanjaro; the European Alps; the Rocky Mountains (North America); and more rarely peaks in Borneo, Irian Jaya, New Zealand, Japan and Hawaii.

Before You Go

Ensure that you have insurance cover for altitude sickness as well as helicopter search and rescue in remoter regions. Check with commercial high altitude trekking agencies what arrangements and equipment they will be providing in case of illness. Appropriate warm clothing, sleeping bags and equipment are essential, as well as a first aid kit, sunglasses (100 per cent UV protection) and suncream. If you have any pre-existing illness (diabetes, asthma, etc.) check with your doctor before travelling.

Minimising Risk of Acute Mountain Sickness (AMS)

Ascent can only be made safe by allowing time to acclimatise and the risk of developing AMS is minimised by keeping two golden rules when above 3000 metres:

Ascend slowly – no more than 300 metres per day, with one rest day every three days or 1000 metres. The rate of ascent is critical – the faster you go up, the more likely you are to become ill. Trekkers who are competitive in ascent are more likely to develop AMS. The height at which you sleep is all important – climbing higher during the day may help acclimatisation as long as the night is spent within the recommended altitude, i.e. *climb high, sleep low*. Plan to cross a high mountain pass early in the day rather than getting stranded at the top as the sun sets. Allow extra rest days to acclimatise, especially if flying directly to a high destination (e.g. Leh, Lukla, Quito, La Paz, Cuzco) or travelling in large groups (not everyone will acclimatise at the same rate). Anybody with symptoms of AMS (see below) should not ascend until further acclimatisation has taken place.

Many people use acetazolamide (*Diamox*) to prevent AMS, in a dosage of 250mg twice a day, starting at least 24 hours before ascent. While this does reduce symptoms of AMS, side effects are not uncommon (including frequent urination – a pain on a cold night – tingling and numbness of fingers, toes and around the mouth and altered taste) and there is no evidence that more serious complications are prevented. Recommendations for safe ascent should not be ignored, Diamox must not be used to enable quicker ascent.

Altitude-Related Illness

Acute Mountain Sickness (AMS)

Upon ascent, nearly all lowlanders will experience some symptoms. These include a throbbing headache, lethargy, nausea and loss of appetite. Sometimes the headache may be severe and associated with vomiting. These are common symptoms and signal that further time to acclimatise is required. The treatment is rest and aspirin or paracetamol: the symptoms will usually resolve with time at this altitude. Do not ascend any further as there is a risk of developing serious complications such as HAPE or HACE (see below). Use of acetazolamide (*Diamox*) in a dose of 250mg three times a day and dexamethasone in a dose of 4mg three times a day reduce symptoms, but if severe (e.g. persistent vomiting, headache not relieved by treatment) immediate descent should be considered.

TRAVELLERS' DISEASES

High Altitude Pulmonary Edema (HAPE) and High Altitude Cerebral Edema (HACE)

HAPE is caused by fluid in the lung, leading to severe breathlessness and cough with frothy sputum, sometimes pink. The lips may become blue. HACE (fluid in the brain) produces severe headache with unsteadiness, confusion, drowsiness and in severe cases convulsions and uncoordination leading to coma. Both are life-threatening complications. DESCEND IMMEDIATELY and seek urgent medical advice. Give oxygen if available. Drug treatment for HAPE is nifedipine (20mg four times a day) and for HACE is dexamethasone (large initial dose (10-15mg) followed by 8mg three times a day). In both cases hyperbaric treatment is useful. Diamox and dexamethasone are given if AMS is also suspected; antibiotics are sometimes given in HAPE. If in doubt, it is always prudent to descend.

Portable Hyperbaric Chambers (Gamow or Certec Bags, or their equivalent)

These are bags into which patients with HAPE or HACE are inserted and air is then pumped in to mimic the effects of descent. They are carried on many commercial treks and can be life-saving.

These chambers should not be used instead of, or to delay descent and if at all possible, always chose descent. Use of the bag buys time rather than curing altitude sickness. People with chest injuries should not be treated (as there is the likelihood of a ruptured lung) and the patient should be able to lie flat and equalise pressure across the ears.

The bag has a zip, a pump fitting an air inlet, two relief valves that trigger at a preset pressure and a clear perspex window. Lie the patient in the bag (preferably on a mat) and zip it shut. Pump rapidly until the wall of the chamber is filled out, then much more slowly, checking every half minute that equalisation is taking place. Once the valves trigger (emitting a hissing sound), continuous pumping is required to cycle fresh air. This is around eight to 12 pumps per minute (one every seven seconds) for the Certec and 12 pumps per minute (one every five to seven seconds) for the Gamow and Certec bags. Arrange a means of communication (walkie-talkie, writing pad or international diving signals) to include 'I'm OK', 'Stop', 'Deflate', etc. Bladder emptying beforehand is essential! Pumping is hard work so recruit volunteers.

Recommended treatment times are one to two hours and should be repeated if the patient remains unwell and descent is still not possible.

Other Related Conditions

Infections

Boil drinking water for longer (two minutes at sea-level, one minute extra for every 300 metres above this) or use a portable water filter or iodine to kill germs. There is anecdotal evidence that skin and respiratory infections are more frequent (especially over 4000 metres) with reduced oxygen. Consider descending if infections linger.

Cold exposure

Cold injury affects the fingers, toes, nose, ears and other areas (e.g. buttocks, cheeks). Prevention with warm gloves (including a dry spare pair) and frequent checking of susceptible areas is essential. Frostnip (white discoloured skin) is characterised by pain followed by a loss of sensation with tingling upon rewarming but full recovery is usual. Frostbite occurs when skin and tissues freeze then swell and mottle purple on rewarming, leading to blisters and black, dead tissue. It is seldom as bad as it looks. Keep the affected part warm (refreezing causes more damage), dry and most importantly, free of infection (bathe in antiseptic). Surgery should be avoided as far as possible. Seek specialist advice.

Hypothermia is also preventable with good equipment

and planning of routes. If it develops, however, stop walking and seek shelter. Replace wet clothing, and use a sleeping bag and head covering to prevent heat loss. Rewarm slowly with warm water bottles or sandwiching between others using sleeping bags zipped together. Dehydration and low blood sugar may be contributing factors so warm, sweet fluids should be given (but never alcohol). Seek help.

Snow blindness

Snow blindness (watery, painful eyes with blurred vision), which is caused by UV light, is preventable using sunglasses with 100 per cent UVB protection. Protect from further damage with sunglasses and rest away from the sun. Take aspirin/paracetamol for pain. Eye drops containing steroids (hydrocortisone, *Predsol*, etc.) or cyclopentolate one per cent will help, and antibiotic drops/ointment will treat infection introduced by eye rubbing.

Children, Pregnant Women and Contraception

Children are no less prone to altitude illness. Indeed, there is anecdotal evidence that those under five years are more at risk of AMS, HAPE and HACE. In addition, they are less likely to complain of specific symptoms and more likely to suffer from cold and dehydration (due to a relatively larger surface area for their size).

Little is known about pregnancy and altitude, but a lowlander should probably avoid going high (above 2000 metres) because of reduced oxygen to the developing foetus. Although data are scant, both oral contraceptives and high altitude itself are associated with a slightly increased risk of thrombosis, and the use of alternative forms of contraception is preferable.

IF YOU CAN'T STAND THE HEAT...

by Sarah Thorowgood

After a particularly long night drive, I once found myself on a beach in the Algarve at nine o'clock in the morning, tired and exhausted after having driven all the way from Granada in Spain in one go. I promptly fell asleep on the then already warm sand until about four in the afternoon. When I awoke, apart from feeling a little groggy, nothing appeared to be amiss. It was only a couple of hours later that the effects of soaking up half the sun's UV rays for an entire day really began to take its toll.

Quite apart from feeling that I could probably radiate enough heat for an entire Mediterranean holiday season, it became quite exceptionally difficult and painful to sit down. Then the blisters came, followed by great lumps of skin that fell off my back for the next two weeks. I was lucky not to suffer more severely from sun stroke, but who knows what untold damage lurks beneath the surface in terms of skin cancer? Some doctors contend that one bad dose of sunburn is all it can take to trigger skin cancer in later life. With the thinning of the ozone layer and greater awareness of the damage that the sun can do to your skin, not to mention an increase annually in the number of people taking summer holidays in hot sunny locations, people are crying out for guidelines as to what is a safe amount of sun and what is not.

Here are a few ways to minimise the risk of sunburn, or anything more sinister:

• The longer term effects of sun on the skin are the signs of ageing and possible skin cancer. Many of the so-called signs of ageing are now thought to be caused directly by sun exposure: just look at the difference in skin texture between the inner and outer parts of your arm.

• Try always to avoid the very strong sun between 11am and 3pm, especially if you are in the tropics.

• Gradually build up your exposure to the sun. A tan gives you a natural protection roughly equivalent to sun protection factor three.

• Use sun screens. These undoubtedly help to protect you from the worst excesses of sun burn, but only up to a limited amount of exposure. There are two different types of sun screen – absorbent and reflective. Absorbent creams only absorb UVB rays. Reflective creams are the type you see Australian cricketers wearing: they have colour in them to reflect every kind of light thrown at them and will protect you from both UVA and UVB rays.

• Sun Protection Factors (SPFs) are merely guides which tell you how long you can stay in the sun without burning. They are a multiple number of the time you could stay in the sun without burning if you were not wearing any protective cream. For example, if it took you 15 minutes to burn in the midday sun without protection, it would take you 4 x 15 minutes to burn in the midday sun if you were wearing SPF 4 (i.e. one hour). After this, reapplication of the same strength cream will not give you any more protection. High protection factor creams may allow you to stay out in the sun longer without burning, but if they are absorbent creams, they can be dangerous, because they will only protect you from UVB rays and will encourage greater exposure to the sun. Children, in particular, are vulnerable, and prolonged exposure to the sun, even if high SPF cream is used, can lead to problems in later life from skin cancer caused by the UVA rays.

Treatment of Sunburn

There are a few ways to relieve the pain of sunburn, but really once you have got to this stage the damage has already been done and you will have to put up with painful and peeling skin for a few days.

Cooling lotion such as Calamine is very soothing and

aspirin is useful for its anti-inflammatory properties. The current medical wisdom is that blisters should not be deliberately punctured, but that if they do puncture, the skin should be peeled away using tweezers sterilised with a flame. Beware of oily creams if your skin is burnt because they will keep the heat trapped inside. Hydrocortisone cream can be useful for very badly burnt areas. Remember that burns have a dehydrating effect, so drink lots of water to replace fluids.

Heat Illness

In hot, dry climates protection from the heat is relatively simple: stay in the shade and drink lots of water. Heat exhaustion and heat stroke are much more likely in tropical, humid environments because it is much harder for the body to cool itself when the sweat it produces does not evaporate (a process which causes cooling).

Heat exhaustion is a problem that will affect people who try to do too much too soon after arriving in the tropics, especially if they are overweight. Give your body a chance to readjust to the new environment before taking exercise.

The Symptoms of Heat Exhaustion

• Excessive sweating – this is the body's attempt to cool down, but it also can cause dehydration and a pounding headache, weakness, muscle cramps, a rapid pulse and vomiting.

• The body also tries to cool down by bringing the blood nearer to the surface of the skin. In temperate conditions this helps to cool the body rapidly, but in the tropics the process will take longer, which means that the brain is getting less blood than normal and fainting may occur.

• The victim may have a temperature of up to 104°F.

Treatment

It is important to act quickly if someone is displaying these symptoms. The first thing to do is to move the person into the coolest place you can find, an air-conditioned room, or just into the shade if there is no other option. Remove the patient's clothes and sponge the body with cool, but not freezing, water. Fan the patient to promote evaporation and give paracetamol to reduce the temperature and help relieve any headache or muscle cramps. If possible, make the person drink lots of water: dehydration is almost certain to have occurred and as much as two or three litres may need to be given in the first hour. Continue to cool the patient until his temperature has dropped to below 100°F or 100.2°F.

The Symptoms of Heat Stroke

This is not as common as heat exhaustion but carries a high mortality if not treated promptly. The symptoms of heat exhaustion may be displayed but they will also be accompanied by:

- A very high temperature, above 104°F.
- Uncoordination, delirium and irrational behaviour.
- A high pulse and respiratory rate.
- Possible convulsions followed by unconsciousness.

Treatment

If the patient falls into unconsciousness, then hospitalisation is needed urgently, because, if not treated quickly, this can lead to permanent disability or death. Treat the patient as you would for symptoms of heat exhaustion, whilst arranging for transfer to hospital. It is important to keep a close eye on the person's temperature, because excessive cooling may even lead to hypothermia. After cooling the victim, cover them up to prevent this from happening.

DISEASES AND THEIR SYMPTOMS
by Drs Sharon Welby and Nick Beeching

This section contains brief outlines of some, but no means all, of the exotic infectious problems that travellers might encounter. They are presented in alphabetical order rather than in order of their importance and for some diseases we felt that the details provided in the *Vaccines* section in Chapter One were sufficient. Diseases listed in italics are sub-sections of the previous listing. Those wishing to explore the diseases in more detail can consult textbooks of tropical medicine or infectious diseases in their local library. More "user friendly" sources of information include the websites of the Centres for Disease Control and the World Health Organisation (**http://www.cdc.gov/** and **http://www.who.org/** web addresses respectively) or Dr. Richard Dawood's book *Travellers' Health: How to Stay Healthy Abroad.*

The risk of contracting many of these infections is extremely small, and few doctors working outside specialist referral centres will have detailed knowledge of most of them. See the percentage risk chart on p. 203, which is based on a large survey of Swiss travellers.

Amoebiasis: Some forms of amoeba acquired via food and water can cause a severe bloody diarrhoea, often without fever. Diagnosis is by stool microscopy, followed by antibiotic treatment (metronidazole or tinidazole). Rarely, and sometimes months after travel, amoebae can cause liver abscesses, characterised by pain below the ribs on the right hand side and high fever. Diagnosis requires an ultrasound scan of the liver and special blood tests, and the condition is easily treated with antibiotics. Amoebic liver abscesses can occur in people who never had symptoms of diarrhoea.

Cholera: See *Vaccines* p. 26.

TRAVELLERS' DISEASES

Cutaneous larva migrans: This occurs in the tropics and subtropics and is particularly common in people visiting the Caribbean. The worm penetrates the unbroken bare skin and causes itchy meandering skin tracks which move about one centimetre a day and may last for months. The lesion is very itchy and occasionally blisters. This is easily treated with topical antihelminth cream or with tablets. The worm is a hookworm which usually infects cats or dogs. The eggs are passed in the animal faeces and contaminate the soil or sand, and infect people whose skin comes into direct contact with the contaminated sand. One couple who decided to bury themselves in the sand in Jamaica ended up with a dozen or more skin tracks each.

Dengue fever: A mosquito transmitted viral infection occurring in tropical and subtropical areas. Epidemic transmission is usually during, and shortly after, the rainy season. Dengue is mainly a disease of urban areas and rarely occurs above 4000 feet. Outbreaks have occurred with increasing frequency over the last 15 years in most countries in the tropics. The risk is greatest in the Indian subcontinent, Southeast Asia, Southern China, Central and South America (except Chile, Paraguay, and Argentina), the Caribbean (except the Cayman Islands), Mexico and Africa.

There is no vaccine but the risk can be reduced by taking measures to reduce mosquito bites. The mosquito that transmits dengue fever is more active during the day time.

Dengue fever used to be known as "breakbone fever" and typically causes a sudden onset of high fever, severe headaches, joint and muscle pain, nausea and vomiting. The fever sometimes falls temporarily after a few days and then recurs. A fine pinpoint red rash appears after three to four days of fever. The illness may last up to ten days and recovery may take two to four weeks. Paracetamol rather than aspirin should be used to relieve symptoms. The more severe forms of dengue haemorrhagic fever or dengue shock syndrome are rare among travellers. Symptoms are initially the same but the illness progresses to faintness, shock and generalised bleeding. The shock syndrome and haemorrhagic syndrome can be treated effectively with fluid replacement in hospital and the mortality is reduced to less than one per cent. The diagnosis is made on antibody blood tests. If fever occurs more than three weeks after leaving an endemic area it is not due to dengue.

Diphtheria: Diphtheria is a bacteria infection which causes a sore throat, occasionally a skin ulcer and produces a powerful toxin. Transmission is by inhalation of infective droplets from the cough of an infected person, or by direct skin contact with infective dust. The incubation period is two to five days followed by a throat infection, often with a thick white membrane which can swell and cause breathing difficulties. The bacteria then produce a powerful toxin which affects the heart and brain (causing heart failure and paralysis respectively). Diphtheria has reached epidemic proportions in Russia and other parts of the former Soviet Union with over 52 000 cases reported in 1995 and 1,700 deaths. A study of blood donors in the UK showed that over a third did not have immunity to diphtheria, with a trend to decreasing immunity with increasing age. Treatment consists of penicillin and antitoxin, and an effective vaccine is available. (See *Vaccines* p. 26.)

Viral encephalitis: Viral encephaltis is a mosquito-borne viral infection which can cause a range of illness from a simple fever to swelling of the brain (encephalitis) causing unconsciousness or alteration in behaviour. For every person that develops the encephalitis, there are many who have unapparent infections or only a mild fever. There is no specific treatment for viral encephalitis but there is a vaccine for Japanese encephalitis (see *Vaccines* p. 28). The risk can also be reduced by avoiding mosquito bites.

Japanese encephalitis (JE): JE is widespread in Asia and the Western Pacific. Many infections are unapparent but in about 0.2 per cent of cases the infection is severe, reaching a mortality rate in elderly people of over 50 per cent. Among people who are bitten by an infected mosquito, only one in 50 to one in 1000 people will develop the illness. The majority of people either develop no illness or a mild illness. However, among those who develop encephalitis, the consequences may be grave. The incubation period is four to 14 days followed by sudden onset of fever, and within 24 hours there are signs of acute neck rigidity, drowsiness and convulsions. After three days coma can result; if the acute stage is survived then recovery is slow. There is a high mortality rate of 25 per cent, and 30 per cent of those that recover have residual paralysis or brain problems. The risk to the average tourist is low – the American Centers for Disease Control (CDC) estimated the risk of JE disease as less than one per million travellers annually. However, the risk is higher if travelling in the rainy season in rural areas where there is coexisting rice and pig farming, and is proportional to the length of time spent in a high risk area.

St Louis encephalitis: This is the most important mosquito-borne virus in the USA. We receive many telephone calls from concerned tourists to Florida following periodic public health alerts about this infection, which occurs there intermittently. Most infections are unapparent in a ratio of 100:1. The incubation period is a few days and symptoms are usually just a fever lasting a few days followed by complete recovery. In a few cases, usually the elderly, encephalitis can develop. Patients usually recover quickly and with no complications.

Tickborne encephalitis: This viral infection occurs in the forested areas of Austria, Germany, Scandinavia, Eastern Europe and Western states of the former USSR. The incubation period is eight to 14 days. The onset of symptoms is generally sudden and consists of fever, severe headache, nausea and photophobia (intolerance of light). The infection is often unapparent, but when overt is severe (three per cent mortality).

The risk of tick bites can be reduced in endemic areas by using insect repellents, tucking trousers into socks and inspecting your skin for ticks. If a tick is detected it should be removed as soon as possible using tweezers to pull the tick gently away from the skin intact. (See *Vaccines* p. 30.)

Filariasis (Bancroftian): This parasite is transmitted by the bite of an infected mosquito and occurs in Central and South America, Africa, the Indian subcontinent and Asia. It is a rare disease in travellers. The adult worms live in the lymph vessels and produce microscopic larvae (called microfilariae) which can be found periodically in the blood. Symptoms include attacks of hot swollen glands, and men may get a hydrocoel (swollen testicle). Chronic infection over a long period of time can lead to swollen limbs (elephantiasis). There is no vaccine but the small risk of disease can be reduced by using insect repellents.

Giardiasis: Giardia is a protozoan parasite that is common everywhere, acquired through contaminated food and water. It typically causes offensive (and explosive) diarrhoea after an incubation period of at least two to three weeks. It is a common cause of prolonged diarrhoea, sometimes with marked weight loss, in travellers to the tropics. It can usually be diagnosed by stool examination and is treated with metronidazole or tinidazole.

Hepatitis: "Hepatitis" means inflammation of the liver, and may be caused by a variety of viruses that attack the liver (hepatitis A, B, C etc.), alcohol, prescribed drugs and many other infections such as glandular fever, dengue and malaria. The symptoms are similar whatever the cause, with jaundice (yellow discolouration of the whites of the eyes, and later the skin), dark urine, pale bowel motions, feeling generally unwell and mild fever. Some people have severe bone and joint pains at the beginning. The precise cause of hepatitis can only be diagnosed by a variety of specific blood tests. Hepatitis A and E are both viruses that are transmitted in food and water in the tropics, with incubation periods of about two to six weeks. Neither causes any lasting liver damage once the acute illness is over. Hepatitis B is transmitted by sex, needles, transfusion etc. (see article on *HIV/AIDS and Sex Abroad* in Chapter Three) and hepatitis C is mainly transmitted by blood products and needles. Both hepatitis B and C can cause continued liver problems. Patients with hepatitis will be ill for at least several weeks, and it can take months for full recovery even after an "uncomplicated" attack. A very small proportion can develop severe liver failure, the danger signs being progressive severe drowsiness (and coma), bleeding from the gums or spontaneous bruising of the skin. The risk of such rare problems rises with age. There is no specific treatment but patients with hepatitis should always seek specific medical advice and should not drink any alcohol while jaundice persists. Both hepatitis A and B can be prevented by vaccination. (See *Vaccines* pp. 26-28.)

Jiggers: These are fleas which are free-living and occur in South America, Africa, and India. The flea attacks man, pigs, poultry and other animals. Adult females burrow in to the skin especially around the nails of the toes but any part of the body can be affected. Once in the skin, the flea swells to the size and shape of a small white pea. Only when the jigger is mature and distended with eggs will it start to irritate, approximately eight to 12 days after infection, when severe inflammation and ulceration occur so that the eggs are expelled. Eggs are discharged into the soil to form larvae and continue the life cycle. Secondary infection of the small ulcers is the chief danger. Fleas should be removed with a needle and delivered whole. To avoid the infection it is best to wear shoes at all times. We regularly see travellers after overland trips who need to have lesions dug out under sterile conditions. It is common for these lesions to get infected, and courses of antibiotics are routinely prescribed after the flea has been removed.

Leishmaniasis: This is caused by a parasite which is transmitted by the bite of sandflies. The disease occurs in Central and South America, Caribbean, Africa, the Indian subcontinent, southern Europe and the USSR. Symptoms include skin sores (cutaneous leishmaniasis), prolonged fever, weakness and a swollen spleen (kalar azar). No vaccine is available but measures to prevent insect bites will reduce the risk of exposure to the parasite. Treatment is available.

Leptospirosis: This infection is caused by a bacteria that infects rats, cows and other animals which then pass the bacteria out in their urine, contaminating fresh water. Risk areas for travellers include countries of South and Central America and Asia. Travellers are infected by contact with water, particularly when canoeing, white-water rafting and wind-surfing, or when wading through rice-paddies on military manoeuvres. Agriculturists and farmers are also at risk, and the infection is widespread in temperate countries as well as in the tropics. Symptoms vary from mild fever with tender muscles to severe jaundice and liver failure, or occasionally a form of meningitis. Diagnosis requires specialist expertise and treatment with antibiotics is required. Severe cases require intensive care facilities for their management. There is no vaccine and prevention with antibiotics is only used in specific epidemic, military or disaster situations.

Lyme disease: The majority of cases of Lyme disease have been reported in the north eastern United States during the summer months but cases have also been reported in the UK, USA, Europe, Australia, Asia and Northern Africa. This is a bacterial infection (*Borrelia burgdorferi*) which is spread by the bite of an infected hard tick. The ticks are usually found in forests and bush areas. The bites often go unnoticed because of the small size of the tick (about the size of a pin head). The incubation period is from three to 30 days and a range of symptoms can occur, some unapparent, others severe. A characteristic rash often occurs at the site of the lesion (erythema chronicum migrans) and may be associated with headache, muscle and joint aches and a slight fever. Treatment is with antibiotics. Left untreated, neurological, joint and cardiac complications may occur. These also respond to a more intensive course of antibiotics.

There is no vaccine available but the risk of disease can be reduced in high risk areas by using insect repellents, tucking trousers into socks and inspecting skin for ticks. If a tick is detected it should be removed as soon as possible using tweezers to pull the tick away intact from the skin.

Malaria: See *Malaria* article in this chapter.

Meningitis: "Meningitis" means inflammation of the lining of the brain and spinal cord and can be caused by viruses and bacteria. Bacterial meningitis is a severe, life-threatening illness, characterised by the rapid onset of nausea, vomiting, fever, severe headache and, with some forms, a progressive purplish rash. The affected patient cannot bear to open their eyes in the light, and will look very ill and have a stiff neck. Untreated, the illness is often fatal, so urgent medical attention and treatment with antibiotics is required. One bacterial cause of meningitis – "meningococcal meningitis" – is common in certain parts of sub-Saharan Africa and the northern Indian subcontinent. Specific pre-travel advice should be sought if travelling to these regions. There is a vaccine to prevent some strains of meningococcal meningitis. (See *Vaccines* p. 28.)

Myiasis: Myiasis is a condition which looks superficially like a boil, but the boil moves and on close inspection two black eyes are looking back at you. The lesion is painful and is due to the larva of the Tumbu fly which is present in Africa. The Tumbu fly lays its eggs on washing that has been put out to dry in the shade. When the contaminated clothing is put on, the larva invades the skin and causes boil-like lesions. Eventually, when the larva has matured after eight to 12 days, it emerges and falls to the ground where it pupates and the adult fly hatches out. Rodents and dogs are the usual host. The best way to get the larva out is to suffocate it with an oily substance like Vaseline. Alternatives include suffocating the larva with bacon strips – both methods have aesthetic draw backs, but are preferable to "digging" operations suggested by some hardier male patients. The infection can be prevented by ironing clothes (this kills the eggs): a friend once commented that the only time she ironed her underwear was when she lived in Africa.

The bot fly causes a similar condition in Central and South America. The eggs hitch a ride on the feet of flies and mosquitoes. When the mosquito takes a bite it leaves behind the egg packets and the larvae burrow into the skin or eye. This causes a painful inflammatory swelling of two to three centimetres. The duration of larva development is about six to 12 weeks. The lesions are found more commonly on the head but can occur elsewhere, and the flies can penetrate clothing. Most larvae have to be removed surgically.

Plague: This occurs in Southeast Asia, South America, Central Africa and Western North America. It is a bacterial infection transmitted by a bite of an infected flea or some-times through exposure to plague-infected animals or their tissues, and through person-to-person spread. Classical plague symptoms include very painful swollen hot glands (bubos), fever and extreme exhaustion. Antibiotic treatment is effective. There is a vaccine against the bubonic type of plague but it is not widely available.

Polio: This viral infection ranges in severity from unapparent infection to fever, gut symptoms, meningitis or paralysis. There are three types of polio virus, each of which can cause clinical infection. The disease is spread from person to person either directly in mucus from the nose or throat, or under poor hygienic conditions when food and drink is contaminated by faeces. The incubation period is three to 21 days.

The symptoms occur in two phases – an initial non-specific illness of fever, headache, muscle pains, gastro-intestinal disturbance, malaise and sometimes stiffness of the neck, followed in some cases after a short interval by the return of muscle pains and the development of paralysis. The paralysis may be limited to a single limb or may spread to involve much of the body. Occasionally death may occur from paralysis of the respiratory muscles. This disease is still a problem in most parts of the tropics but can be prevented by vaccination. (See *Vaccines* p. 29.)

Rabies: See *Vaccines* p. 29 and *Rabies* in this chapter.

Tetanus: This infection is caused by bacteria which produce a toxin that damages the muscle and nervous system. The bacteria live in the guts of humans and animals where they do not cause disease, but excrete spores in the faeces which then contaminate the environment. The spores are widely distributed in dust and soil (especially if treated with manure), and can also contaminate unsterilised medical instruments. The disease is spread by contamination of wounds, burns and even trivial puncture injuries with these spores. The incubation period is from four to 21 days. The symptoms usually start with spasm of the jaw known as "lockjaw" and progress to muscle rigidity and spasms. Death can occur during a spasm. Those that recover have a long and painful convalescence. (See *Vaccines* p. 30.)

Trypanosomiasis

African Trypanosomiasis (sleeping sickness): African trypanosomiasis occurs in West, Central and East Africa. This parasite is transmitted by the bite of an infected tsetse fly. Symptoms include a swelling at the site of the bite, followed by fever, headaches and severe illness. In West Africa the initial infection is usually symptomless with sleeping sickness developing after a few years and manifesting itself in daytime sleepiness and behavioural and mood changes. Travellers are rarely infected, the main risk is during safari and the risk can be reduced by using insect repellents. No vaccine is available.

American Trypanosomiasis (Chagas' disease): This disease is transmitted by blood-sucking bugs (known as reduviid bug, cone nosed or kissing bugs) or by blood transfusions, and occurs in Central and South America. These bugs live in the mud walls and thatched roofs of buildings and feed at night. The initial infection can be unapparent, or may produce swelling around the eye or lumps under the skin, followed by a fever and swollen glands a few weeks later. If people are not treated the disease can progress after many years to cause heart disease and gut problems. Infection can be avoided by not staying overnight in buildings possibly contaminated with the bugs and, if possible, by avoiding blood transfusions in endemic countries. There is no vaccine and treatment is limited.

TRAVELLERS' DISEASES

Tuberculosis (TB): Tuberculosis affects millions of people in the tropics and is on the increase again world-wide, particularly in HIV positive individuals. TB affects people in many ways, but the usual illness is a progressive pneumonia, characterised by a long-lasting cough producing sputum (sometimes blood-stained), fever, wasting and ultimately death if untreated ("consumption"). The disease is passed on by breathing in bacteria in aerosols created by infected people coughing, and exposure to such patients in crowded, poverty-associated conditions carries a high risk. Drinking unpasteurised cow milk is also risky in the tropics, as it may harbour the bacteria. TB is not a major risk for most travellers, but health-care workers and others working in refugee situations, for example, are at some risk.

Diagnosis requires medical expertise, chest X-rays and special sputum tests, followed by prolonged supervised treatment with a combination of specific antibiotics. Most British people are vaccinated at entry to secondary school (BCG) but this is not established practice in some countries, notably the USA, because the vaccine is only partially protective. (See *Vaccines* p. 30.)

Typhoid ("enteric fever"): Typhoid and paratyphoid are similar illnesses, caused by certain salmonella bacteria that are transmitted in contaminated food and water. The infection is found world-wide, wherever water supplies are inadequate, but the most important risk area for the traveller is the Indian subcontinent and the Far East. The illness starts with non-specific, sustained fever that gets worse over a week and is accompanied by headache, extreme lethargy and sometimes confusion. Some patients develop a pinpoint skin rash after the first week of illness and patients may have diarrhoea, or, later, constipation. Untreated, the illness lasts about three weeks and about ten per cent of people have severe complications, especially bowel perforation. It is diagnosed by culture of blood samples, and is easily treated with appropriate antibiotics. Unfortunately, most typhoid acquired in the Indian subcontinent and in Asia is resistant to the older antibiotics, but it still responds to quinolone antibiotics such as ciprofloxacin and ofloxacin. Typhoid is preventable by immunisations and care with food and water. (See *Vaccines* p. 31.)

Typhus: True typhus is very rare and presents little danger for most travellers. It is caused by small organisms known as *rickettsiae* which are similar to bacteria. There are many other types of typhus transmitted by different vectors (such as ticks, body lice, mites and rat fleas). The symptoms consist of fever, severe headache and skin rash, and sometimes a black scab (eschar) occurs at the site of the tick bite. The severity of illness varies between the different types of typhus. The treatment involves antibiotics and there is no vaccine available.

Tick and Scrub Typhus: Tick typhus occurs in Africa, America, Asia and the Pacific islands and Scrub typhus occurs in Asia and the Pacific islands. Tick typhus presents a significant hazard to travellers on Safari in many parts of Africa. Scrub typhus can be a severe infection and travellers may be infected by the bite of mites which live in areas of "scrub" vegetation, also known as areas of "transitional" or "secondary" vegetation.

The risk of tick and mite bites can be reduced in endemic areas by using insect repellents, tucking trousers into socks and inspecting skin for ticks. If a tick is detected it should be removed as soon as possible using tweezers to pull the tick away intact from the skin.

Viral haemorrhagic fevers: (Lassa Fever, Rift Valley Fever, Ebola and Marburg disease). These diseases occur in Africa, and are caused by viruses transmitted from an infected person or animal to another person, by mosquitoes or food contaminated with rat's urine. Congo-Crimean haemorrhagic fever is more widespread in Asia. These diseases are not a significant health problem to most travellers unless they are healthcare workers or travelling rough in very rural areas, but they can cause severe illness. Treatment is limited and no vaccines are available.

Worms: Worm infections occur world-wide but they are more common when living under poor hygienic conditions. Human faeces containing worm eggs contaminate the soil, food and water. Another person swallows the contaminated food or water and an adult worm develops. Usually there are no symptoms and the eggs are discovered during screening tests of stool specimens or occasionally they just surprise people and wiggle their way out of the rectum. Recently, we saw a medical student who was distressed after passing a fine specimen of roundworm a year after working in Sri Lanka and India. Most worms are easily treated with tablets. Some worm larvae go on a safari through the body shortly after hatching in the gut, and can cause respiratory symptoms of wheezing and shortness of breath. This usually settles after a few weeks and there is no specific treatment.

Yellow fever: This is a viral infection transmitted by the bite of infected mosquitoes. The disease occurs in Central and West Africa, parts of South America and Panama. The incubation period is three to seven days and the illness ranges in severity from mild symptoms to death. The mortality rate can be as much as 50 per cent. The initial symptoms are fever, vomiting and prostration, which may progress to liver failure with jaundice and haemorrhage. There is a very effective vaccination and only recently the risks of travelling unimmunised was highlighted by two unfortunate travellers who died from yellow fever after visiting Brazil. (See *Vaccines* p. 31.)

DIRECTORY

WORLD-WIDE HEALTH PROFILE

This country by country health profile is intended to give you an initial starting point for geographical and health information about the country you intend to visit.

Key

Lang lists the official, and other, languages spoken throughout the country.
GMT states the time difference in relation to Greenwich Mean Time.
Pop lists the latest available population figures.
Density of population measured in number of people per square kilometre.
Life Exp Life expectancy for Males first then Females.
Safety a guide to the political and social stability at time of going to press: for up to date information contact the Foreign Office Travel Advice Unit.
Med Care a guide to the standard and extent of free medical care available. Whilst there are reciprocal health agreements between some countries (e.g. members of the European Community), insurance is nevertheless recommended. See also the *Medical Insurance* article in Chapter One.

Afghanistan

Capital Kabul *Lang* Pashtu and Dari, some English spoken *GMT* + 4.5 *Pop* 17,080,000 *Density* 25.7 *Life Exp* **M** 41 **F** 42 *Safety* Dangerous at present, strict Muslim majority therefore women should not travel alone and should be totally covered, outside Kabul in tribal areas very little protection. At present politically unstable – check with Foreign Office *Med Care* very limited and up-front cash payments necessary, medical insurance strongly recommended.

Albania

Capital Tirana *Lang* Albanian but Greek is also spoken *GMT* + 1 *Pop* 3,363,000 (+2 in summer) *Density* 117 *Life Exp* **M** 69.3 **F** 75.4 *Safety* armed guerrilla gangs still operating in the south of the country, Tirana is calmer – check with Foreign Office

Med Care medical treatment to be paid for except infectious diseases, medical insurance recommended.

Algeria

Capital Algiers (El Djezair) *Lang* Arabic and French *GMT* + 1 *Pop* 26,581,000 *Density* 11.2 *Life Exp* **M** 64.1 **F** 65 *Safety* High risk area, in the last three years there have been many attacks on westerners. Curfew between 23.30 and 04.00 *Med Care* basic in rural areas and medical insurance strongly recommended.

American Samoa (US)

Capital Pago Pago *Lang* Samoan and English *GMT* – 11 *Pop* 53,000 *Density* 272 *Life Exp* **M** 71 **F** 75 *Safety* Safe *Med Care* good but insurance recommended.

Andorra

Capital Andorra La Vella *Lang*

Officially Catalan, but French and Spanish also used *GMT* +1 *Pop* 65,227 (+2 in summer) *Density* 130.6 *Life Exp* M 74 F 81 *Safety* Safe *Med Care* good and covered by mutual agreements with UK.

Angola

Capital Luanda *Lang* Officially Portuguese and Bantu languages *GMT* +1 *Pop* 1,609,000 *Density* 8.5 *Life Exp* M 42.4 F 45.6 *Safety* volatile situation – check with Foreign Office *Med Care* free but generally inadequate, medical insurance recommended for evacuation.

Anguilla (UK)

Capital The Valley *Lang* English *GMT* -4 *Pop* 10,300 *Density* 93.3 *Life Exp* M 71 F 77 *Safety* Safe *Med Care* one hospital on island, free treatment for minor ailments but insurance recommended.

Antigua and Barbuda

Capital St John's *Lang* English *GMT* -4 *Pop* 64,166 *Density* 142.5 *Life Exp* 74 *Safety* Safe *Med Care* one private and one public hospital, insurance recommended.

Argentina

Capital Buenos Aires *Lang* Spanish *GMT* -3 *Pop* 34,180,000 *Density* 12.1 *Life Exp* M 67.6 F 74 *Safety* beware of pickpockets, register with British Embassy *Med Care* good but no health agreements with UK so insurance recommended.

Armenia (C.I.S.)

Capital Yerevan *Lang* Armenian and Russian *GMT* +3 *Pop* 3,354,000 *Density* 125.6 *Life Exp* 73.9 *Safety* political and religious unrest with Azberbaijan, tourists strongly advised not to go to any Trans-Causican republic, and to register with relevant embassy in Yerevan *Med Care* arrangement for urgent medical treatment exists for those with proof of UK citizenship but standards are low and insurance is recommended.

Aruba (The Netherlands)

Capital Oranjestad *Lang* Dutch but English and Spanish are also spoken *GMT* -4 *Pop* 80,333 *Density* 434.8 *Life Exp* M 71.1 F 77.1 *Safety* Safe *Med Care* good facilities at the one hospital on the island but insurance recommended.

Australia

Capital Canberra *Lang* English *GMT* +8-+10 *Pop* 17,657,400 *Density* 2.3 *Life Exp* M 74.1 F 80.4 *Safety* Relatively safe *Med Care* free hospital treatment for UK citizens in emergencies only, insurance recommended.

Austria

Capital Vienna *Lang* German *GMT* +1 *Pop* 8,031,100 *Density* 96 *Life Exp* M 72.9 F 79.4 *Safety* Safe *Med Care* free treatment for UK citizens in emergency with nominal fee, a refund may be available for treatment in private hospitals.

Azerbaijan (C.I.S)

Capital Baku *Lang* Azerbaijani *GMT* + 4 *Pop* 7,499,000 *Density* 85 *Life Exp* M 66.6 F 74.2 *Safety*

Although cease-fire in place since May 1994, the western area of the country is still volatile. Street crime increasing in all cities *Med Care* limited but free emergency treatment for a limited period only, insurance recommended.

Bahamas

Capital Nassau *Lang* English *GMT* -5 (-4 in summer) *Pop* 269,000 *Density* 18.7 *Life Exp* M 68.3 F 75.3 *Safety* Safe *Med Care* four hospitals where medical costs are high, insurance recommended.

Bahrain

Capital Manama *Lang* Arabic and English *GMT* +3 *Pop* 568,063 *Density* 775.7 *Life Exp* M 68.8 F 72.9 *Safety* Safe *Med Care* good and free emergency medical treatment.

Bangladesh

Capital Dhaka *Lang* Bengali and English *GMT* +6 *Pop* 117,787,000 *Density* 755 *Life Exp* M 56.9 F 56 *Safety* Safe if sensible, women should be covered *Med Care* limited and basic, insurance strongly recommended.

Barbados

Capital Bridgetown *Lang* English *GMT* -4 (-5 in summer) *Pop* 264,000 *Density* 61.8 *Life Exp* M 71.9 F 76.9 *Safety* Don't carry any valuables, mugging on the increase *Med Care* UK citizens entitled to free hospital treatment but medicines for anyone other than children and the elderly must be paid for.

Belarus

Capital Minsk *Lang* Belarussian *GMT* +2 *Pop* 10,297,000 *Density* 49.6 *Life Exp* M 66.8 F 76.4 *Safety* Seek local advice *Med Care* free hospital treatment for UK citizens but medicines may be unobtainable, insurance recommended.

Belgium

Capital Brussels *Lang* Flemish and French *GMT* +1 *Pop* 10,100,631 *Density* 331 *Life Exp* 77.2 *Safety* Safe *Med Care* UK citizens with E111 certificate entitled to a 75 per cent refund on medical costs.

Belize

Capital Belmopan *Lang* English *GMT* -6 *Pop* 209,000 *Density* 9 *Life Exp* M 69.9 F 71.8 *Safety* Mugging and theft occur, but not as bad as South America *Med Care* cash payments will generally be demanded for all treatment, insurance strongly recommended.

Benin

Capital Porto Novo *Lang* French and indigenous tribal languages *GMT* +1 *Pop* 5,215,000 *Density* 43.1 *Life Exp* M 43.9 F 47.1 *Safety* Poorly lit roads make night travel hazardous. Armed robbery and muggings are on the increase *Med Care* very limited and cash payments expected, insurance strongly recommended.

Bermuda

Capital Hamilton *Lang* English *GMT* -4 *Pop* 59,549 *Density* 1123.5 *Life Exp* M 68.6 F 76.3 *Safety* Safe *Med Care* good but medical costs are high, insurance strongly recommended.

Bhutan

Capital Thimphu *Lang* Dzongkha *GMT* +6 *Pop* 600,000 *Density* 13 *Life Exp* M 45.6 F 46.6 *Safety* safe *Med Care* basic, insurance strongly recommended.

Bolivia

Capital La Paz *Lang* Spanish *GMT* -4 *Pop* 7,237,000 *Density* 6.6 *Life Exp* M 56.6 F 61.2 *Safety* Care should be taken, theft can be rife. The cocaine growing areas should be avoided *Med Care* basic in public hospitals, insurance strongly recommended.

Bonaire (Netherland Antilles)

Capital Kralendjik *Lang* Dutch *GMT* -4 *Pop* 10,187 *Density* 35 *Life Exp* M 71.1 F 75.6 *Safety* safe *Med Care* minor cases dealt with on the island and there is an air ambulance service to Curaçao for more serious problems, insurance recommended.

Bosnia-Herzegovina

Capital Sarajevo *Lang* Serb-Croat and Croat-Serb *GMT* +1 *Pop* 3,527,000 *Density* 72.5 *Safety* Extremely dangerous – despite peace agreement, land mines and violence still a hazard *Med Care* very limited, insurance with repatriation cover recommended.

Botswana

Capital Gaborone *Lang* English and Setswana *GMT* +2 *Pop* 1,450,000 *Density* 2.5 *Life Exp* M 55.5 F 61.5 *Safety* safe *Med Care* there is a nominal fee for hospital care and medicines supplied by government hospitals are free but outside towns health facilities are basic and insurance is recommended.

Brazil

Capital Brasilia *Lang* Portuguese *GMT* from -3 to -5 *Pop* 155,822,440 *Density* 19.1 *Life Exp* M 64.9 F 67.6 *Safety* As with all countries in South America beware of pickpockets *Med Care* no health agreements with UK and medical costs are high, insurance strongly recommended.

Brunei

Capital Bandar Seri Begawan *Lang* Malay and English *GMT* +8 *Pop* 284,500 *Density* 47.9 *Life Exp* M 72.4 F 76.2 *Safety* safe *Med Care* good but repatriation may be necessary for certain treatments so insurance recommended.

Bulgaria

Capital Sofia *Lang* Bulgarian *GMT* +2 *Pop* 8,427,418 *Density* 76.2 *Life Exp* M 67.6 F 74.4 *Safety* Beware of their driving habits *Med Care* free health care for UK citizens, some specialised treatments may not be available.

Burkina Faso

Capital Ouagadougou *Lang* French and several indigenous *GMT*: GMT *Pop* 9,889,000 *Density* 35.3 *Life Exp* M 45.3 F 48.8 *Safety* Towns can be violent after dark, avoid unnecessary travel in rural areas *Med Care* limited, basic remedies should be bought before entering the country and insurance is strongly recommended including air evacuation cover.

Burundi

Capital Bujumbura *Lang* French and Kirundi *GMT* +2 *Pop* 6,134,000 *Density* 214.1 *Life Exp* M 46.7 F 50.1 *Safety* Unsafe due to tribal tension and recent coup – contact Foreign Office *Med Care* limited and payment will be demanded, insurance strongly recommended.

Cambodia

Capital Phnom Penh *Lang* Khmer – Chinese and Vietnamese also spoken *GMT* +7 *Pop* 9,568,000 *Density* 51.4 *Life Exp* M 49.4 F 52.2 *Safety* unsafe, fighting and kidnapping still a serious risk, the presence of unexploded mines makes travel off the beaten track very dangerous *Med Care* limited and immediate cash payments demanded, insurance strongly recommended.

Cameroon

Capital Yaounde *Lang* French and English *GMT* +1 *Pop* 11,540,000 *Density* 24.3 *Life Exp* M 52 F 55 *Safety* Douala can be dangerous after dark *Med Care* basic outside cities, insurance recommended.

Canada

Capital Ottawa *Lang* French and English *GMT* from -3.5 to -8 *Pop* 29,248,000 *Density* 2.9 *Life Exp* M 75.1 F 81.1 *Safety* Safe *Med Care* good but expensive, insurance recommended.

Cape Verde

Capital Cidade de Praia *Lang* Portuguese *GMT* -1 *Pop* 341,491 *Density* 84.7 *Life Exp* M 65 F 67 *Safety* safe *Med Care* very limited and expensive, insurance recommended.

Cayman Islands (UK)

Capital George Town *Lang* English *GMT* -5 *Pop* 32,000 *Density* 127.4 *Safety* Safe *Med Care* good but insurance recommended.

Central African Republic

Capital Bangui *Lang* French and Sango *GMT* +1 *Pop* 2,463,616 *Density* 5.0 *Life Exp* M 47.2 F 50.6 *Safety* Volatile – contact Foreign Office. Represented only by honorary British Consulate, contact French or German Embassies in emergencies *Med Care* very limited, take own basic medical supplies and full insurance.

Chad

Capital Ndjamena *Lang* French, Arabic and 50 indigenous langs. *GMT* +1 *Pop* 6,214,000 *Density* 4.8 *Safety* Dangerous contact High Commission in Abuja *Med Care* very limited, take own supply of basic medicines and full insurance cover.

Chile

Capital Santiago *Lang* Spanish *GMT* -6 *Pop* 14,210,429 *Density* 18.5 *Life Exp* M 68.1 F 75.1 *Safety*

DIRECTORY

Safe *Med Care* good but insurance necessary.

China
Capital Beijing *Lang* Mandarin Chinese *GMT* +8 *Pop* 1,198,500,000 *Density* 123.8 *Life Exp* M 66.4 F 69.4 *Safety* Safe *Med Care* good but some medicines may be unavailable, insurance recommended.

Colombia
Capital Santa Fe de Bogotá *Lang* Spanish *GMT*-5 *Pop* 34,520,000 *Density* 30.2 *Life Exp* M 63.4 F 69.2 *Safety* Violence and kidnapping remain a serious problem. Do not accept food, sweets or drinks from strangers, they may be drugged *Med Care* limited outside cities.

Comoros
Capital Moroni *Lang* French and Arabic *GMT* +3 *Pop* 484,000 *Density* 255.1 *Life Exp* M 53 F 55.9 *Safety* safe *Med Care* full insurance recommended.

Congo
Capital Brazzaville *Lang* French *GMT* +1 *Pop* 1,843,421 *Density* 5.4 *Life Exp* M 49.4 F 54.7 *Safety* UK nationals at risk – contact Foreign Office for up to date info. *Med Care* limited, insurance strongly recommended.

Cook Islands (New Zealand)
Capital Avarua on the island Rarotonga *Lang* Maori, English also spoken *GMT* -10 *Pop* 19,000 *Density* 78.3 *Life Exp* M 70 F 73 *Safety* Safe *Med Care* good but check with tourist office to see if free medical care agreement between UK and NZ applies here.

Costa Rica
Capital San Jose *Lang* Spanish *GMT* -7 *Pop* 3,500,000 *Density* 63.3 *Life Exp* M 73.1 F 77.7 *Safety* Beware of tides while swimming *Med Care* good and free hospital treatment in emergencies, but insurance recommended.

Côte d'Ivoire (Ivory Coast)
Capital Yamoussoukro *Lang* French *GMT* GMT *Pop* 13,695,000 *Density* 43.1 *Life Exp* M 50.3 F 53.7 *Safety* Generally safe but has its full share of street crime after dark *Med Care* fair, but insurance recommended.

Croatia
Capital Zagreb *Lang* Croat-Serb and Serb-Croat *GMT* +1 *Pop* 4,779,000 *Density* 84.5 *Life Exp* M 71 F 77.8 *Safety* Earth tremors in Southern Croatia, border areas are dangerous – consult Foreign Office *Med Care* free hospital care for UK citizens, some payment for medication may be demanded.

Cuba
Capital Havana *Lang* Spanish *GMT* -4 *Pop* 10,901,000 *Density* 98.3 *Life Exp* M 73.5 F 77 *Safety* Be aware of bag snatchers *Med Care* limited, insurance recommended in case of need for repatriation.

Curaçao
(Netherlands Antilles)
Capital Willemstad *Lang* Dutch *GMT* -4 *Pop* 144,097 *Density* 324.5 *Life Exp* M 71.1 F 75.8 *Safety* safe *Med Care* good but expensive so insurance recommended.

Cyprus (Southern part of island)
Capital Nicosia *Lang* Greek *GMT* +2 *Pop* 729,800 *Density* 78.1 *Life Exp* M 74.6 F 79.1 *Safety* safe *Med Care* good, but insurance recommended.

Czech Republic
Capital Prague *Lang* Czech *GMT* +1 *Pop* 10,333,616 *Density* 131 *Life Exp* M 68.2 F 76.1 *Safety* safe *Med Care* free for UK citizens.

Denmark
Capital Copenhagen *Lang* Danish *GMT* +1 (+2 in summer) *Pop* 5,215,718 *Density* 120.6 *Life Exp* M 72.3 F 77.6 *Safety* Safe *Med Care* very good and free for UK citizens.

Djibouti
Capital Djibouti *Lang* Arabic and French *GMT* +3 *Pop* 519,900 *Density* 22.4 *Life Exp* M 45.4 F 48.6 *Safety* Areas in the country remain closed. Risk of banditry at night *Med Care* insurance highly recommended.

Dominica
Capital Roseau *Lang* English *GMT* -4 *Pop* 71,183 *Density* 94.9 *Life Exp* 72 *Safety* Safe *Med Care* cash payments demanded, insurance strongly recommended.

Dominican Republic
Capital Santo Domingo *Lang* Spanish *GMT* -4 *Pop* 7,769,000 *Density* 160 *Life Exp* M 63.9 F 68.1 *Safety* safe *Med Care* insurance recommended.

Ecuador
Capital Quito *Lang* Spanish *GMT* -5 (Galapagos Islands -6) *Pop* 11,460,117 *Density* 41.2 *Life Exp* M 63.4 F 67.6 *Safety* Ecuador is one of the safest countries in South America but still be on your guard, violent crime increasing in all areas *Med Care* good but expensive, insurance recommended.

Egypt
Capital Cairo *Lang* Arabic *GMT* +2 *Pop* 57,581,000 *Density* 57.7 *Life Exp* M 62.9 F 66.39 *Safety* An increase of attacks on tourist by religious extremists *Med Care* insurance strongly recommended.

El Salvador
Capital San Salvador *Lang* Spanish *GMT* -6 *Pop* 5,047,925 *Density* 243.6 *Life Exp* M 50.7 F 63.9 *Safety* Robbery and murder are not uncommon, for advice contact Embassy in San Salvador *Med Care* cash payments demanded, insurance strongly recommended.

Equatorial Guinea
Capital Malbabo *Lang* Spanish *GMT* +1 *Pop* 356,000 *Density* 12.7 *Life Exp* M 44.4 F 47.6 *Safety* Exercise caution. There is no British Consular presence. If in difficulties seek assistance from the French or Spanish Embassies *Med*

Care limited, insurance cover for repatriation recommended.

Eritrea

Capital Asmara *Lang* Arabic and Tigrinya *GMT* +3 *Pop* 3,435,500 *Density* 28.2 *Life Exp* 46 *Safety* Avoid Sudan border. Don't travel after dark. Register with the Consulate in Asmara if travelling outside the capital *Med Care* adequate but insurance strongly recommended.

Estonia

Capital Tallinn *Lang* Estonian *GMT* +2 (+3 in summer) *Pop* 1,476,301 *Density* 33.3 *Life Exp* M 64.1 F 75 *Safety* Safe *Med Care* limited and cash payments demanded, insurance recommended.

Ethiopia

Capital Addis Ababa *Lang* Amharic *GMT* +3 *Pop* 56,677,100 *Density* 47.3 *Life Exp* M 43.4 F 46.6 *Safety* Sudan and Somalia border areas should be avoided. Do not travel after dark and register with an Embassy if travelling outside the capital by road *Med Care* limited, repatriation cover recommended.

Falkland Islands (UK)

Capital Stanley *Lang* English *GMT* -4 (-3 in winter) *Pop* 2,050 *Density* 0.17 *Life Exp* M 68.2 F 73.8 *Safety* Safe, except there are marked unexploded mines left over from the war, seek local advice *Med Care* free for UK residents.

Fiji

Capital Suva *Lang* Fijian and Hindi

GMT +12 *Pop* 797,078 *Density* 43.6 *Life Exp* M 68.3 F 72.5 *Safety* Safe *Med Care* adequate but insurance recommended.

Finland

Capital Helsinki *Lang* Finnish *GMT* +2 *Pop* 5,098,754 *Density* 15 *Life Exp* M 72.8 F 80.2 *Safety* Safe *Med Care* UK citizens eligible for a refund on most medical expenses.

France

Capital Paris *Lang* French *GMT* +1 *Pop* 57,903,000 *Density* 106 *Life Exp* M 73.1 F 81.3 *Safety* Safe *Med Care* UK citizens eligible for a refund on some medical expenses.

French Guiana (France)

Capital Cayenne *Lang* French *GMT* -3 *Pop* 114,808 *Density* 1.3 *Life Exp* M 62.3 F 67.6 *Safety* safe *Med Care* as for France but limited.

Gabon

Capital Liberville *Lang* French *GMT* +1 *Pop* 1,011,710 *Density* 3.8 *Life Exp* M 49.9 F 53.2 *Safety* Generally stable but elections cause tension – check with Foreign Office *Med Care* very limited, insurance strongly recommended.

The Gambia

Capital Banjul *Lang* English *GMT* GMT *Pop* 1,038,145 *Density* 90.8 *Life Exp* M 41.4 F 44.6 *Safety* Calm since military coup of 1994, but check with Foreign Office *Med Care* adequate, insurance advised, take supplies of basic medicines.

Georgia

Capital Tbilisi *Lang* Georgian,

Russian *GMT* +4 *Pop* 5,471,000 *Density* 78.5 *Life Exp* M 68.1 F 75.7 *Safety* Avoid travel at night outside Tbilisi – contact Foreign Office *Med Care* limited but free emergency care for UK citizens.

Germany
Capital Berlin *Lang* German *GMT* +1 *Pop* 81,338,093 *Density* 228 *Life Exp* M 71.7 F 78.2 *Safety* Safe *Med Care* free to UK citizens, with charge for prescribed medicines.

Ghana
Capital Accra *Lang* English *GMT* GMT *Pop* 17,000,000 *Density* 64.6 *Life Exp* M 52.2 F 55.8 *Safety* Precautions should be taken, travel after dark not recommended *Med Care* adequate but insurance recommended.

Gibraltar
Capital Gibraltar *Lang* English and Spanish *GMT* +1 *Pop* 28,051 *Density* 4,315.5 *Life Exp* M 73.4 F 80.4 *Safety* Safe *Med Care* free to UK citizens.

Greece
Capital Athens *Lang* Greek *GMT* +2 *Pop* 10,368,600 *Density* 77.1 *Life Exp* M 74.9 F 80.2 *Safety* Safe *Med Care* refunds for hospital care can be obtained from IKA offices in Greece, but it will not be for more than 50 per cent at the most, insurance strongly recommended.

Greenland
Capital Nuuk *Lang* Greenlandic *GMT* -4 *Pop* 55,732 *Density* 0.025 *Life Exp* M 58.8 F 68.1 *Safety* Safe

Med Care can be difficulties in obtaining supplies, but care is free for UK citizens.

Grenada
Capital St Georges *Lang* English *GMT* -4 *Pop* 94,806 *Density* 276.7 *Life Exp* 71 *Safety* safe *Med Care* adequate, but insurance recommended because relocation to mainland may be necessary and payment demanded for all treatment.

Guadeloupe
Capital Basse-Terre (admin) Pointe-a-Pitre (comm) *Lang* French *GMT* -4 *Pop* 387,034 *Density* 217.4 *Life Exp* M 70.1 F 77.1 *Safety* safe *Med Care* generally, as for France but check with embassy.

Guam (US)
Capital Agana *Lang* English and Chamorro *GMT* +10 *Pop* 146,000 *Density* 273.2 *Life Exp* 72 *Safety* Safe *Med Care* limited, and as for USA, insurance strongly recommended.

Guatemala
Capital Guatemala City *Lang* Spanish *GMT* -6 *Pop* 10,322,011 *Density* 94.8 *Life Exp* M 59.7 F 64.4 *Safety* Beware of fighting between guerrillas and government soldiers *Med Care* limited outside capital and all healthcare has to be paid for.

Guinea Republic
Capital Conakry *Lang* French *GMT* GMT *Pop* 5,600,000 *Density* 22.8 *Life Exp* M 42.5 F 43 *Safety* High levels of violent street crime.

DIRECTORY

Leave valuables in secure place *Med Care* limited and all health treatments must be paid for, insurance recommended.

Guinea-Bissau
Capital Bissau *Lang* Portuguese *GMT* GMT *Pop* 1,050,000 *Density* 29.1 *Life Exp* M 42.5 F 43 *Safety* check with Foreign Office *Med Care* limited and immediate payment expected, insurance strongly recommended.

Guyana
Capital Georgetown *Lang* English *GMT* -3 *Pop* 737,947 *Density* 3.4 *Life Exp* M 60.4 F 66.1 *Safety* Violent crime common in Georgetown *Med Care* limited supplies and hospital care, insurance recommended.

Haiti
Capital Port-au-Prince *Lang* French and Creole *GMT* -5 *Pop* 7,041,000 *Density* 253.7 *Life Exp* M 53.1 F 56.4 *Safety* political unrest – check with Foreign Office *Med Care* unreliable, insurance strongly recommended.

Honduras
Capital Tegucigalpa *Lang* Spanish *GMT* -6 *Pop* 5,770,000 *Density* 51.5 *Life Exp* M 61.9 F 66.1 *Safety* Violence has increased, do not wear jewellery or carry large amounts of cash *Med Care* limited, insurance strongly recommended.

Hong Kong
Capital Hong Kong *Lang* Chinese and English *GMT* +8 *Pop* 6,189,800 *Density* 5790 *Life Exp* M 75.4 F 81.0 *Safety* Safe *Med Care* very good, but insurance strongly recommended.

Hungary
Capital Budapest *Lang* Hungarian *GMT* +1 *Pop* 10,276,968 *Density* 110.5 *Life Exp* M 65 F 73.8 *Safety* Safe *Med Care* free health care for UK citizens.

Iceland
Capital Reykjavik *Lang* Icelandic *GMT* GMT *Pop* 267,809 *Density* 2.6 *Life Exp* M 75 F 80.8 *Safety* Safe *Med Care* very good, insurance recommended.

India
Capital New Delhi *Lang* English *GMT* +5.5 *Pop* 920,000,000 *Density* 264.7 *Life Exp* M 57.8 F 57.9 *Safety* Safe if sensible, certain areas, e.g. Jammu and Kashmir, in state of unrest and should be avoided, kidnapping a serious risk *Med Care* limited and insurance strongly recommended.

Indonesia
Capital Jakarta *Lang* Bahasa Indonesian *GMT* +7 – +9 *Pop* 194,440,100 *Density* 100.5 *Life Exp* M 58.5 F 62 *Safety* Petty crime attacks on foreigners have increased, also kidnap by OPM is a risk in Irian Jaya *Med Care* limited outside cities, insurance with repatriation cover recommended.

Iran
Capital Tehran *Lang* Persian (Farsi) *GMT* +3.5 *Pop* 59,778,000 *Density* 36.2 *Life Exp* M 65 F 65.5

Safety Take sensible precautions, there is a total ban on video cameras, women should be completely covered up *Med Care* very limited outside capital, insurance recommended.

Iraq
Capital Baghdad *Lang* Arabic *GMT* +3 *Pop* 17,903,000 *Density* 40.8 *Life Exp* M 77.4 F 78.2 *Safety* The Foreign Office do not recommend any visits to Iraq *Med Care* limited and insurance cover with repatriation strongly recommended.

Ireland (Eire)
Capital Dublin *Lang* English and Gaelic *GMT* GMT *Pop* 3,582,200 *Density* 51 *Life Exp* M 72.7 F 78.2 *Safety* Safe *Med Care* free to UK citizens.

Israel
Capital Jerusalem *Lang* Hebrew and Arabic *GMT* +2 *Pop* 5,462,200 *Density* 236.8 *Life Exp* M 74.9 F 78.5 *Safety* Mainly safe, but unrest in certain areas, take local advice *Med Care* very good but insurance recommended.

Italy
Capital Rome *Lang* Italian *GMT* +1 *Pop* 57,268,578 *Density* 188.4 *Life Exp* M 73.7 F 80.2 *Safety* Safe *Med Care* good but free treatment for emergencies only, insurance recommended.

Jamaica
Capital Kingston *Lang* English *GMT* -5 *Pop* 2,374,193 *Density* 216 *Life Exp* M 70.4 F 74.8 *Safety* Generally safe for tourists but be vigilant, do not walk at night or use public transport *Med Care* adequate but insurance recommended.

Japan
Capital Tokyo *Lang* Japanese *GMT* +9 *Pop* 125,200,000 *Density* 329.4 *Life Exp* M 75.9 F 81.8 *Safety* Safe *Med Care* very good but expensive, insurance strongly recommended.

Jordan
Capital Amman *Lang* Arabic *GMT* +2 *Pop* 5,198,000 *Density* 42.3 *Life Exp* M 64.2 F 67.8 *Safety* Safe *Med Care* good but insurance recommended.

Kazakhstan
Capital Almaty *Lang* Kazakh *GMT* +5 (+6 in summer) *Pop* 16,763,000 *Density* 6.2 *Life Exp* M 63.9 F 73.1 *Safety* Increase in attacks on trains and in larger cities, travel in groups *Med Care* varies and supplies may be limited, insurance with repatriation cover recommended.

Kenya
Capital Nairobi *Lang* Swahili and English *GMT* +3 *Pop* 29,292,000 *Density* 36.9 *Life Exp* M 55.9 F 59.9 *Safety* Generally safe in tourist areas, but care should be taken *Med Care* adequate but insurance recommended.

Korea (North)
Capital Pyongyang *Lang* Korean *Currency* Won = 100 jon *GMT* +9 *Pop* 23,483,000 *Density* 191.3 *Life Exp* M 66.2 F 72.7 *Med Care* generally good, but supplies may be limited, insurance recommended.

DIRECTORY

Korea (South)
Capital Seoul *Lang* Korean *GMT* +9 *Pop* 44,850,801 *Density* 439.7 *Life Exp* M 66.9 F 75 *Safety* Safe *Med Care* adequate but payment demanded, insurance recommended.

Kuwait
Capital Kuwait City *Lang* Arabic and English *GMT* +3 *Pop* 1,575,983 *Density* 90.9 *Life Exp* M 72.6 F 76.3 *Safety* The border with Iraq should be avoided, and care should be taken in more remote spots for unexploded ordnance *Med Care* free emergency treatment at state medical centre but otherwise very expensive, insurance strongly recommended.

Kyrgyzstan (C.I.S.)
Capital Bishkek *Lang* Kyrgyz *GMT* +5 *Pop* 4,476,400 *Density* 22.6 *Life Exp* M 64.3 F 72.4 *Safety* mostly safe, theft a problem *Med Care* limited and cash payments demanded, insurance essential.

Laos
Capital Vientiane *Lang* Laotian *GMT* +7 *Pop* 4,581,258 *Density* 19.4 *Life Exp* M 49.3 F 52.3 *Safety* safe *Med Care* limited and cash payments demanded, insurance strongly recommended.

Latvia
Capital Riga *Lang* Latvian *GMT* +2 *Pop* 2,529,500 *Density* 39.7 *Life Exp* M 61.6 F 73.8 *Safety* Safe *Med Care* limited and expensive, insurance strongly recommended.

Lebanon
Capital Beirut *Lang* Arabic *GMT* +2 *Pop* 3,855,000 *Density* 271.5 *Life Exp* M 65.1 F 69 *Safety* Unstable, check with Foreign Office *Med Care* adequate, but insurance recommended.

Lesotho
Capital Maseru *Lang* Sesotho and English *GMT* +2 *Pop* 1,700,000 *Density* 63.7 *Life Exp* M 55.5 F 60.5 *Safety* Travel with caution *Med Care* cash payments, insurance recommended.

Liberia
Capital Monrovia *Lang* English *GMT* GMT *Pop* 2,700,000 *Density* 27 *Life Exp* M 52 F 54 *Safety* The British Embassy in Liberia was closed in 1991. The Foreign Office do not advise travel. *Med Care* very limited, insurance with repatriation cover recommended.

Libya
Capital Tripoli *Lang* Arabic *GMT* +1 *Pop* 4,899,000 *Density* 2.6 *Life Exp* M 59.1 F 62.5 *Safety* Avoid internal air flights. Incidence of mugging increasing. Unwise to carry cameras. Harsh penalties are imposed for the possession or use of alcohol or drugs and for criticising the country, its leadership or religion. Register with the British Interests Section of the Italian Embassy on arrival *Med Care* limited outside capital, insurance strongly recommended.

Liechtenstein
Capital Vaduz *Lang* German *GMT* +1 *Pop* 30,629 *Density* 189 *Life Exp* M 78 F 84 *Safety* Safe *Med*

Care very good and free for UK citizens.

Lithuania

Capital Vilnius *Lang* Lithuanian *GMT* +2 *Pop* 3,717,700 *Density* 56.9 *Life Exp* M 63.3 F 75 *Safety* Safe *Med Care* free emergency treatment, but insurance recommended.

Luxembourg

Capital Luxembourg-ville *Lang* German *GMT* +1 *Pop* 406,600 *Density* 155 *Life Exp* M 72.6 F 79.1 *Safety* Safe *Med Care* good and refunds can be obtained for all but medical basic costs.

Macau

Capital Macau *Lang* Portuguese and Chinese *GMT* +8 *Pop* 400,000 *Density* 20,482 *Life Exp* M 70.1 F 75.7 *Safety* Safe *Med Care* good but insurance recommended.

Macedonia (Former Yugoslav Republic of Macedonia)

Capital Skopje *Lang* Macedonian *GMT* + 1 *Pop* 1,936,877 *Density* 75.3 *Life Exp* M 71 F 74 *Safety* Seek advice from the Foreign Office *Med Care* emergency treatment free but repatriation insurance cover recommended.

Madagascar

Capital Antananarivo *Lang* Malagasy and French *GMT* + 3 *Pop* 12,092,157 *Density* 20.6 *Life Exp* M 52 F 55 *Safety* Be aware of mugging danger. Register presence at the Embassy *Med Care* limited and repatriation insurance cover recommended.

Malawi

Capital Lilongwe *Lang* English *GMT* +2 *Pop* 10,032,600 *Density* 84.7 *Life Exp* M 44.6 F 46.2 *Safety* Avoid travelling after dark, especially off the main towns *Med Care* very basic, take supplies with you, insurance with repatriation cover recommended.

Malaysia

Capital Kuala Lumpur *Lang* Bahasa Malaysia *GMT* +8 *Pop* 20,103,000 *Density* 60.3 *Life Exp* M 69 F 73.7 *Safety* Safe *Med Care* good but insurance recommended.

Maldives

Capital Malé *Lang* Dhivehi *GMT* +5 *Pop* 244,644 *Density* 800 *Life Exp* M 66.2 F 65.2 *Safety* Safe *Med Care* adequate but repatriation insurance cover recommended.

Mali

Capital Bamako *Lang* French *GMT* GMT *Pop* 8,156,000 *Density* 6.6 *Life Exp* M 42.4 F 45.6 *Safety* Many areas north of Bamako are unsafe due to clashes between Tuareg and army *Med Care* very limited, take medical supplies with you, insurance with repatriation cover strongly recommended.

Malta

Capital Valletta *Lang* Maltese *GMT* +1 *Pop* 369,451 *Density* 1,168 *Life Exp* M 74.7 F 78.6 *Safety* Safe *Med Care* good and free for UK citizens.

DIRECTORY

Martinique (France)

Capital Fort-de-France *Lang* French *GMT* -4 *Pop* 370,800 *Density* 326.6 *Life Exp* **M** 72 **F** 78.7 *Safety* safe *Med Care* generally as for France but check with embassy.

Mauritania

Capital Nouakchott *Lang* Arabic and French *GMT* GMT *Pop* 2,211,000 *Density* 2 *Life Exp* **M** 44.4 **F** 47.6 *Safety* Disputes with Senegal, contact Foreign Office *Med Care* limited and insurance with repatriation cover recommended.

Mauritius

Capital Port Louis *Lang* English *GMT* +4 *Pop* 1,112,607 *Density* 538.2 *Life Exp* **M** 66.8 **F** 73.9 *Safety* Safe *Med Care* good but insurance recommended.

Mexico

Capital Mexico City *Lang* Spanish *GMT* -6 to -8 *Pop* 93,008,000 *Density* 46 *Life Exp* **M** 65.7 **F** 72.1 *Safety* Central Chaipas remains tense, seek local advice *Med Care* good, but insurance recommended.

Moldova

Capital Chisinau *Lang* Romanian *GMT* +2 *Pop* 4,350,000 *Density* **129.3** *Life Exp* **M** 65.5 **F** 72.3 *Safety* Seek advice from the Foreign Office before travelling *Med Care* free emergency treatment but supplies may be limited, insurance recommended.

Monaco

Capital Monaco-ville *Lang* French *GMT* +1 *Pop* 29,972 *Density* 15,321 *Life Exp* **M** 73.1 **F** 81.3 *Safety* Safe *Med Care* good but expensive, insurance strongly recommended.

Mongolia

Capital Ulan Bator *Lang* Mongolian Khalkha *GMT* +8 *Pop* 2,317,000 *Density* 1.5 *Life Exp* 62.5 *Safety* There is some street-crime in Ulan Bator *Med Care* limited, insurance with repatriation cover recommended.

Montserrat (UK)

Capital Plymouth *Lang* English *GMT* -4 *Pop* 10,581 *Density* 104.3 *Life Exp* **M** 70.1 **F** 77.1 *Safety* safe *Med Care* limited facilities, free emergency care for those under 16 or over 65, otherwise insurance recommended.

Morocco

Capital Rabat *Lang* Arabic *GMT* GMT *Pop* 26,023,717 *Density* 36.7 *Life Exp* **M** 59.1 **F** 62.5 *Safety* Safe for tourists, beware of drugs being offered *Med Care* good in cities and free for emergency treatment, otherwise insurance recommended.

Mozambique

Capital Maputo *Lang* Portuguese *GMT* +2 *Pop* 17,423,000 *Density* 19.5 *Life Exp* **M** 44.5 **F** 47.8 *Safety* Not recommended for the tourist, great care should be taken at all times *Med Care* limited, insurance with repatriation cover recommended.

Myanmar (Burma)

Capital Yangon (Rangoon) *Lang* Burmese *GMT* +6.5 *Pop*

41,550,000 *Density* 61.4 *Life Exp* M 60 F 63.5 *Safety* Unstable, check with Foreign Office. Tourists are required to keep to officially designated areas *Med Care* adequate but no free facilities, insurance recommended.

Namibia

Capital Windhoek *Lang* English *GMT* +2 *Pop* 1,500,000 *Density* 1.8 *Life Exp* M 55 F 57.5 *Safety* Relatively safe *Med Care* adequate but no free treatment, insurance recommended.

Nepal

Capital Kathmandu *Lang* Nepali *GMT* + 5.45 *Pop* 19,280,081 *Density* 125.4 *Life Exp* M 51.5 F 50.3 *Safety* Safe *Med Care* adequate in capital but no free treatment, insurance recommended.

The Netherlands

Capital Amsterdam *Lang* Dutch *GMT* +1 *Pop* 15,385,000 *Density* 453 *Life Exp* M 74.2 F 80.2 *Safety* Safe *Med Care* good and free treatment for UK citizens.

New Caledonia (France)

Capital Noumena *Lang* French *GMT* +11 *Pop* 183,000 *Density* 9.4 *Life Exp* 70 *Safety* Safe *Med Care* adequate but insurance recommended.

New Zealand

Capital Wellington *Lang* English *GMT* +12 *Pop* 3,592,000 *Density* 13.2 *Life Exp* M 73.4 F 79.1 *Safety* Safe *Med Care* good and free state emergency medical treatment.

Nicaragua

Capital Managua *Lang* Spanish *GMT* -6 *Pop* 4,500,000 *Density* 37.4 *Life Exp* M 64.8 F 67.7 *Safety* political stability and safety can not be guaranteed, contact Foreign Office *Med Care* limited, insurance recommended.

Niger

Capital Niamey *Lang* French *GMT* +1 *Pop* 8,361,000 *Density* 6.6 *Life Exp* M 42.9 F 46.1 *Safety* Potentially unstable: check with Foreign Office *Med Care* very limited, bring own supplies, insurance with repatriation cover recommended.

Nigeria

Capital Abuja *Lang* English *GMT* +1 *Pop* 88,514,501 *Density* 95.8 *Life Exp* M 48.8 F 52.2 *Safety* Political situation is uncertain. High incidence of street crime and business fraud. Travelling outside cities after dark is unsafe *Med Care* very limited except for a few private hospitals in cities, insurance essential.

Norway

Capital Oslo *Lang* Norwegian *GMT* +1 *Pop* 4,348,410 *Density* 13.4 *Life Exp* M 74.2 F 80.3 *Safety* Safe *Med Care* good, mostly free, total refunds for all medical treatment unlikely, insurance advisable.

Oman

Capital Muscat *Lang* Arabic and English *GMT* +4 *Pop* 2,096,000 *Density* 9.5 *Life Exp* M 66.7 F 67.5 *Safety* Safe *Med Care* good but expensive, insurance recommended.

Pakistan

Capital Islamabad *Lang* Urdu and English *GMT* +5 *Pop* 126,610,000 *Density* 152.7 *Life Exp* **M** 56.5 **F** 56.5 *Safety* Safe if sensible in northern areas, however central and south Pakistan are unsafe and advice should be taken *Med Care* limited, cash payments demanded, insurance strongly recommended.

Panama

Capital Panama City *Lang* Spanish *GMT* -5 *Pop* 2,613,586 *Density* 34.2 *Life Exp* **M** 90.1 **F** 74.1 *Safety* Do not visit the Colombian border. Muggings have increased in tourist areas *Med Care* free emergency treatment, insurance recommended.

Papua New Guinea

Capital Port Moresby *Lang* English and Pidgin English *GMT* +10 *Pop* 3,997,000 *Density* 8.5 *Life Exp* **M** 53.2 **F** 54.7 *Safety* Extremely dangerous – take local advice, Port Moresby has gangland violence *Med Care* very limited and cash payments demanded, it may be worthwhile getting a visa for Australia in case of medical emergencies, so that you can be evacuated to decent medical facilities, insurance strongly recommended.

Paraguay

Capital Asuncion *Lang* Spanish and Guarani *GMT* -4 *Pop* 4,642,624 *Density* 11.4 *Life Exp* **M** 64.8 **F** 69.1 *Safety* safe *Med Care* adequate, insurance strongly recommended.

Peru

Capital Lima *Lang* Spanish and Quechua *GMT* -5 *Pop* 23,088,000 *Density* 18 *Life Exp* **M** 62.9 **F** 66.6 *Safety* Extremely dangerous in places, especially the central highlands. Tourists in the past have been attacked by the Shining Path (the terrorist organisation) *Med Care* cash payments demanded, insurance strongly recommended.

Philippines

Capital Manila *Lang* Filipino *GMT* +8 *Pop* 67,038,000 *Density* 206.7 *Life Exp* **M** 63 **F** 66.8 *Safety* Some areas unstable, take local advice *Med Care* adequate three tier system but insurance recommended.

Poland

Capital Warsaw *Lang* Polish *GMT* +1 *Pop* 38,609,000 *Density* 126.5 *Life Exp* **M** 67.4 **F** 76 *Safety* Safe *Med Care* free to UK citizens, except for a charge for 30 per cent of prescribed medicines.

Portugal

Capital Lisbon *Lang* Portuguese *GMT* GMT *Pop* 9,902,200 *Density* 106.9 *Life Exp* **M** 70.8 **F** 78.6 *Safety* Safe *Med Care* good and free for UK citizens.

Puerto Rico (USA)

Capital San Juan *Lang* Spanish *GMT* -4 *Pop* 3,720,000 *Density* 411.3 *Safety* Beware of pickpockets *Med Care* good but expensive, insurance strongly recommended.

Qatar

Capital Doha *Lang* Arabic *GMT*

+3 *Pop* 593,000 *Density* 48.9 *Life Exp* M 66.9 F 71.8 *Safety* safe *Med Care* good but expensive, insurance recommended.

Reunion (France)

Capital Saint-Denis *Lang* French *GMT* +4 *Pop* 642,200 *Density* 251.1 *Life Exp* M 69 F 76.3 *Safety* Safe *Med Care* as for France.

Romania

Capital Bucharest *Lang* Romanian *GMT* +2 *Pop* 22,730,622 *Density* 95.7 *Life Exp* M 66.6 F 73.1 *Safety* Bag snatching on the increase, beware of bogus policemen *Med Care* limited, free for UK citizens except for medicine from chemist.

Russian Federation

Capital Moscow *Lang* Russian *GMT* +3 to +12 *Pop* 148,000,000 *Density* 8.7 *Life Exp* M 63.5 F 74.3 *Safety* Moscow and St Petersburg both have a high crime rate, take local advice, areas like Chechnia are extremely dangerous *Med Care* free emergency treatment but very expensive if further treatment is needed, insurance strongly recommended.

Rwanda

Capital Kigali *Lang* Kinyarwanda and French Kiswahili *GMT* +2 *Pop* 7,164,994 *Density* 272 *Life Exp* M 45.1 F 47.7 *Safety* Security still unstable, police and judicial systems yet to be fully restored *Med Care* extremely limited, insurance with repatriation cover strongly recommended.

Saba (Netherlands Antilles)

Capital The Bottom *Lang* English and Dutch *GMT* -4 *Pop* 1,130 *Density* 86.9 *Life Exp* M 71.1 F 75.8 *Safety* safe *Med Care* one hospital on the island, insurance recommended with evacuation cover.

St Eustatius

Capital Oranjestad *Lang* English *GMT* -4 *Pop* 1,839 *Density* 87.6 *Life Exp* M 71.1 F 75.5 *Safety* safe *Med Care* only one hospital, insurance with evacuation cover recommended.

St Kitts and Nevis

Capital Basseterre *Lang* English *GMT* -4 *Pop* 44,380 *Density* 168.2 *Life Exp* M 65.9 F 71 *Safety* safe *Med Care* adequate but insurance recommended with evacuation cover.

St Lucia

Capital Castries *Lang* English *GMT* -4 *Pop* 139,908 *Density* 220.2 *Life Exp* M 69.3 F 74 *Safety* Safe *Med Care* adequate but expensive, insurance recommended with evacuation cover.

St Maarten

Capital Philipsburg *Lang* English *GMT* -4 *Pop* 32,221 *Density* 785.9 *Life Exp* M 71.1 F 75.8 *Safety* safe *Med Care* good but insurance recommended, with evacuation cover.

St Vincent and Grenadines

Capital Kingstown *Lang* English *GMT* -4 *Pop* 111,000 *Density* 280 *Life Exp* M 69.3 F 74 *Safety* Safe *Med Care* adequate but insurance recommended with evacuation cover.

São Tomé e Principe
Capital São Tomé *Lang* Portuguese *GMT* GMT *Pop* 125,000 *Density* 121.9 *Life Exp* 67 *Safety* safe *Med Care* poor, insurance with evacuation cover strongly recommended.

Saudi Arabia
Capital Riyadh *Lang* Arabic *GMT* +3 *Pop* 16,929,294 *Density* 7.6 *Life Exp* M 59.1 F 62.5 *Safety* Safe *Med Care* of a very high standard but expensive, insurance recommended.

Senegal
Capital Dakar *Lang* French and Wolof *GMT* GMT *Pop* 8,152,000 *Density* 41.4 *Life Exp* M 46.3 F 48.3 *Safety* Some unrest, take local advice *Med Care* basic in rural areas, insurance recommended.

Seychelles
Capital Victoria (Mahé) *Lang* Creole *GMT* +4 *Pop* 74,000 *Density* 158.6 *Life Exp* M 65.3 F 74.1 *Safety* Safe *Med Care* adequate but insurance recommended.

Sierra Leone
Capital Freetown *Lang* English *GMT* GMT *Pop* 4,509,000 *Density* 61 *Life Exp* M 39.4 F 42.6 *Safety* Dangerous, military coup again supplanting brief democratic civilian government, contact the Foreign Office before departing *Med Care* extremely limited, insurance with repatriation cover recommended.

Singapore
Capital Singapore *Lang* Chinese *GMT* +8 *Pop* 2,986,500 *Density* 4677.8 *Life Exp* M 73.7 F 78.3 *Safety* Safe *Med Care* good but expensive, insurance recommended.

Slovak Republic
Capital Bratislava *Lang* Slovak *GMT* +1 *Pop* 5,367,800 *Density* 108 *Life Exp* M 68.4 F 76.3 *Safety* Relatively safe *Med Care* free emergency treatment for UK citizens.

Slovenia
Capital Ljubljana *Lang* Slovene *GMT* +1 *Pop* 1,989,477 *Density* 98.2 *Life Exp* M 69.4 F 77.3 *Safety* Safe *Med Care* good and free emergency treatment for UK citizens.

Solomon Islands
Capital Honiara *Lang* English *GMT* +11 *Pop* 366,000 *Density* 12.9 *Life Exp* M 67.2 F 71.2 *Safety* Safe *Med Care* adequate, but insurance recommended with evacuation cover.

Somalia
Capital Mogadishu *Lang* Somali and Arabic *GMT* +3 *Pop* 7,691,000 *Density* 12.1 *Life Exp* M 43.4 F 46.6 *Safety* Very dangerous – all embassies are currently closed, fierce fighting in the capital *Med Care* very limited, take own medical supplies and insurance with repatriation cover.

South Africa
Capital Pretoria *Lang* Afrikaans and English *GMT* +2 *Pop* 41,244,000 (including the homelands) *Density* 33.1 *Life Exp* M

57.5 **F** 63.5 *Safety* Variable, depends on area, take advice *Med Care* good and free for pregnant women and children, otherwise insurance recommended.

Spain
Capital Madrid *Lang* Spanish *GMT* +1 *Pop* 39,188,194 *Density* 77.5 *Life Exp* **M** 73.8 **F** 80 *Safety* safe *Med Care* good, limited free emergency treatment service, insurance recommended.

Sri Lanka
Capital Colombo *Lang* Sinhala, Tamil and English *GMT* +6 *Pop* 18,000,000 *Density* 273.4 *Life Exp* **M** 67.8 **F** 71.7 *Safety* Mainly safe, take local advice, tension between Tamil Tigers and security forces, but central and south of island largely unaffected *Med Care* free emergency treatment at government hospitals.

Sudan
Capital Khartoum *Lang* Arabic *GMT* +2 *Pop* 24,940,683 *Density* 10 *Life Exp* **M** 48.6 **F** 51 *Safety* Not advised to travel anywhere in the south or Ethiopian and Eritrean borders – contact Foreign Office *Med Care* limited outside capital, insurance strongly recommended.

Suriname
Capital Paramaribo *Lang* Dutch *GMT* -3 *Pop* 418,000 *Density* 2.5 *Life Exp* **M** 66.4 **F** 71.3 *Safety* safe *Med Care* good but expensive, insurance recommended.

Swaziland
Capital Mbabane *Lang* English and Siswati *GMT* +2 *Pop* 879,000 *Density* 47.4 *Life Exp* **M** 53.7 **F** 57.3 *Safety* generally stable but growing number of attacks on expatriates *Med Care* good private health care, insurance recommended.

Sweden
Capital Stockholm *Lang* Swedish *GMT* +1 *Pop* 8,839,000 *Density* 19.4 *Life Exp* **M** 75.7 **F** 80.8 *Safety* Safe *Med Care* very good and free to UK citizens.

Switzerland
Capital Bern *Lang* German *GMT* +1 *Pop* 7,019,019 *Density* 168.8 *Life Exp* **M** 74.7 **F** 81.4 *Safety* Safe *Med Care* good but very expensive, insurance strongly recommended.

Syria
Capital Damascus *Lang* Arabic, French and English *GMT* +2 *Pop* 15,000,000 *Density* 74.6 *Life Exp* **M** 64.4 **F** 68.1 *Safety* Care should be taken to behave appropriately, photography near military bases and government installations is prohibited *Med Care* emergency treatment free to those who cannot afford to pay, insurance recommended.

Taiwan
Capital Taipei *Lang* Mandarin Chinese and English *GMT* +8 *Pop* 21,125,792 *Density* 581.8 *Life Exp* **M** 72 **F** 77.4 *Safety* Safe *Med Care* good but may be expensive, insurance recommended.

DIRECTORY

Tajikistan
Capital Dushanbe *Lang* Tajik *GMT* +5 *Pop* 5,751,000 *Density* 40.2 *Life Exp* M 66.8 F 71.7 *Safety* Terrorism a risk and there is no British mission – check with US or German Embassies before travelling *Med Care* limited, take medical supplies and insurance with you.

Tanzania
Capital Dodoma *Lang* Swahili and English *GMT* +3 *Pop* 30,340,000 *Density* 27.1 *Life Exp* M 50.1 F 53.5 *Safety* more stable now, but mugging and theft common *Med Care* adequate supplies and care at private or religious hospitals but can be expensive, insurance strongly recommended.

Thailand
Capital Bangkok *Lang* Thai *GMT* +7 *Pop* 60,000,000 *Density* 115 *Life Exp* M 63.8 F 68.9 *Safety* Safe apart from border with Myanmar *Med Care* good but insurance recommended.

Togo
Capital Lomé *Lang* French *GMT* GMT *Pop* 3,928,000 *Density* 66.3 *Life Exp* M 51.3 F 54.8 *Safety* Quiet at the moment, but potentially unstable, be vigilant *Med Care* limited, bring own medical supplies and insurance with repatriation cover.

Tonga
Capital Nuku'alofa *Lang* Tongan and English *GMT* +13 *Pop* 98,000 *Density* 131 *Life Exp* 68 *Safety* Safe *Med Care* adequate for minor problems, but insurance with evacuation cover strongly recommended.

Trinidad and Tobago
Capital Port of Spain *Lang* English *GMT* -4 *Pop* 1,249,738 *Density* 245.7 *Life Exp* M 67.7 F 72.7 *Safety* safe *Med Care* free and adequate on Trinidad, but limited on Tobago so insurance recommended.

Tunisia
Capital Tunis *Lang* Arabic *GMT* +1 *Pop* 8,947,100 *Density* 53.3 *Life Exp* M 69 F 71 *Safety* Relatively safe *Med Care* adequate, but all medical supplies to be paid for and they are expensive, consider taking supplies with you and insurance recommended.

Turkey
Capital Ankara *Lang* Turkish *GMT* +2 *Pop* 61,644,000 *Density* 78.5 *Life Exp* M 62.8 F 68 *Safety* Dangerous in the east and southern east provinces, contact the Foreign Office for advice. Western and Central Turkey has seen attacks on tourists by the PKK *Med Care* good but no free health provision, insurance recommended.

Turkmenistan
Capital Ashgabat *Lang* Turkmen *GMT* +5 *Pop* 4,483,300 *Density* 8.7 *Life Exp* M 61.8 F 68.4 *Safety* check with Foreign Office *Med Care* limited, take own supplies with you as well as insurance with repatriation cover.

Turks and Caicos (UK)
Capital Cockburn Town *Lang*

English *GMT* -5 *Pop* 14,000 *Density* 28.7 *Safety* safe *Med Care* free to UK citizens under 16 or over 65 and free prescribed medicine and ambulance travel to all UK citizens, otherwise, insurance recommended.

Tuvalu
Capital Funafuti *Lang* Tuvalaun and English *GMT* +12 *Pop* 9,000 *Density* 348 *Life Exp* M 68.3 F 72.5 *Safety* Safe *Med Care* good but insurance recommended with evacuation cover.

Uganda
Capital Kampala *Lang* English *GMT* +3 *Pop* 16,671,705 *Density* 69.1 *Life Exp* M 43.2 F 46.1 *Safety* armed robbery and road ambushes throughout Uganda. Do not travel at night *Med Care* limited, bring medical supplies with you and insurance with repatriation cover.

Ukraine
Capital Kiev *Lang* Ukrainian *GMT* +2 *Pop* 51,728,400 *Density* 86.2 *Life Exp* M 64 F 69 *Safety* Carjacking and mugging on the increase – be vigilant *Med Care* limited, take supplies with you and full insurance.

United Arab Emirates
Capital Abu Dhabi *Lang* Arabic *GMT* +4 *Pop* 2,377,700 *Density* 28.7 *Life Exp* M 68.6 F 72.9 *Safety* Safe *Med Care* good and free emergency treatment, but any other kind of treatment is very expensive so insurance recommended.

United Kingdom
Capital London *Lang* English *GMT* GMT *Pop* 58,394,600 *Density* 240.7 *Life Exp* M 72.7 F 78.3 *Safety* Safe *Med Care* free emergency treatment for travellers.

United States of America
Capital Washington DC *Lang* English *GMT* -5 to -10 *Pop* 264,648,291 *Density* 26.5 *Life Exp* M 72.1 F 78.9 *Safety* Depends on the area, take local advice, especially in Florida *Med Care* good, but insurance strongly recommended as some hospitals will not treat patients without proof of insurance cover and medical costs are high.

Uruguay
Capital Montevideo *Lang* Spanish *GMT* -3 *Pop* 3,167,000 *Density* 17.9 *Life Exp* M 68.9 F 75.3 *Safety* generally safe, but check with Foreign Office *Med Care* good, but insurance recommended.

Uzbekistan
Capital Tashkent *Lang* Uzbek *GMT* +5 *Pop* 22,098,000 *Density* 48.5 *Safety* Dress down and avoid travelling at night *Med Care* limited, but free for emergency treatment, insurance with repatriation cover strongly recommended.

Vanuatu
Capital Port Vila *Lang* Bislama *GMT* +12 *Pop* 165,000 *Density* 12.8 *Life Exp* 63 *Safety* Safe *Med Care* adequate but insurance strongly recommended.

Venezuela

Capital Caracas *Lang* Spanish *GMT* -4 *Pop* 21,377,000 *Density* 22.7 *Life Exp* **M** 66.7 **F** 72.8 *Safety* Violent crime increasing in cities, register with British Embassy in Caracas *Med Care* good and free emergency treatment for travellers.

Vietnam

Capital Hanoi *Lang* Vietnamese *GMT* +7 *Pop* 70,982,000 *Density* 214.4 *Life Exp* **M** 60.6 **F** 64.8 *Safety* Travel in some areas is dangerous, seek local advice *Med Care* generally limited, insurance with repatriation cover strongly recommended.

Virgin Islands (UK)

Capital Road Town *Lang* English *GMT* -4 *Pop* 19,000 *Density* 108.8 *Life Exp* **M** 72.9 **F** 74.9 *Safety* Safe *Med Care* free for UK citizens.

Virgin Island (US)

Capital Charlotte Amalie *Lang* English *GMT* -4 *Pop* 101,809 *Density* 286.9 *Safety* Safe *Med Care* as for USA.

Yemen

Capital Sana'a *Lang* Arabic *GMT* +3 *Pop* 14,561,330 *Density* 27 *Safety* Security improved but still volatile areas, check with relevant embassy *Med Care* adequate, but insurance recommended.

Yugoslavia (Montenegro and Serbia)

Capital Belgrade *Lang* Serbo-Croat *GMT* +1 *Pop* 10,482,000 *Density* 102.6 *Life Exp* 71.1 *Safety* Avoid Croatian border, car theft and mugging have increased, register with relevant embassy *Med Care* poor and limited supplies, cash payments demanded, insurance with repatriation cover essential.

Democratic Rep. of Congo (Zaïre)

Capital Kinshasa *Lang* Officially French, many African languages used *GMT* +1 and +2 depending on region *Pop* 36,672,000 *Density* 15.6 *Life Exp* **M** 49.8 **F** 53.3 *Safety* Check with Foreign Office, the east should still be treated as a war zone *Med Care* limited and there is a shortage of supplies, insurance with repatriation cover recommended.

Zambia

Capital Lusaka *Lang* English *GMT* +2 *Pop* 8,210,000 *Density* 11.5 *Life Exp* **M** 47.7 **F** 49.5 *Safety* Travellers should be vigilant *Med Care* limited and cash payments demanded, take own supplies, insurance with repatriation cover strongly recommended.

Zimbabwe

Capital Harare *Lang* English *GMT* +2 *Pop* 11,215,000 *Density* 26.6 *Life Exp* **M** 55.1 **F** 56.8 *Safety* Safe *Med Care* good, but insurance recommended.

Further Reading: *World Travel Health Guide* (Columbus Press)

VACCINATION AND INFORMATION CENTRES

In the UK, most vaccinations can be given by the traveller's own doctor. Yellow fever vaccine can be given by some general practitioners, or this and other unusual vaccines can be obtained from the centres listed below. Most vaccines for travel will have to be paid for by the traveller and some, such as Japanese encephalitis, are expensive. Consult your own doctor before ringing any of the hospital-based clinics. WEXAS members can obtain a discount of £5 at the British Airways travel clinics listed below if they spend more than £10.

Vaccination requirements are listed in the *Country by Country Malaria Risk and Vaccination Guide*. Please note these are only guidelines as inoculations can change with new outbreaks of diseases, so please check with your own doctor or with a travel clinic as far in advance as possible.

Centers for Disease Control Traveller's Health section
Tel: **404-332 4559**
Based in Atlanta, they run a 24-hour automated system giving advice by region and on special problems such as malaria, food, water precautions and advice for pregnant travellers.

Central Public Health Laboratory
61 Colindale Avenue
Colindale
London NW9 5HT
Tel: **0181-200 4400**
Provides advice and supplies of rabies vaccines and supplies of gammaglobulin to general practitioners for immunisation against hepatitis A.

Convenience Care Centers
Suite 100
10301 East Darvey
Armani
CA 91733
USA
Undertakes all necessary vaccinations.

Department of Health
Public Enquires Office
Richmond House
79 Whitehall
London SW1A 2NS
Tel: **0171-210 4850**
Also publish a free booklet Health Advice for Travellers. *Call Tel: 0800-555777 to order.*

Department of Infectious Diseases and Tropical Medicine
Birmingham Heartlands Hospital
Bordesley Green East
Birmingham B9 5SS
Tel: **0121-766 6611**
Pre-travel telephone advice and

DIRECTORY

expertise in investigation and treatment of tropical illness.

Department of Infectious Diseases and Tropical Medicine
North Manchester General Hospital
Delaunays Road
Manchester M8 5AB
Tel: **0161-795 4567**

Department of Infectious Diseases and Tropical Medicine/Travel Information
Ruchill Hospital
Glasgow G20 9NB
Tel: **0141-946 7120**
Together with Communicable Disease (Scotland) Unit, provides telephone advice for general practitioners and other doctors and maintains "Travax", a computerised database on travel medicine that may be accessed remotely by modem. Pre- and post-travel clinics and limited travel health supplies. Enquiries/referrals to clinics are best initiated by your general practitioner.

Fleet Street Travel Clinic
29 Fleet Street
London EC4Y 1AA
Tel: **0171-353 5544**
Run by Dr. Richard Dawood, who writes a regular Traveller's Health column for TRAVELLER magazine.

Health Control Unit
Terminal 3 Arrivals
Heathrow Airport
Hounslow
Middlesex TW6 1NB
Tel: **0181-745 7209**

Can give at any time up-to-date information on compulsory and recommended immunisations for different countries.

Hospital for Tropical Diseases
4 St. Pancras Way
London NW1 0PE
Tel: **0171-637 6099** (Travel clinic)
Comprehensive range of pre-travel immunisations and advice, and post–travel check-ups in travel clinic and large travel shop. Pre-recorded healthline gives country-specific health hazards — you will be asked to dial the international dialling code of the relevant country, so have it ready. Centre for investigation and treatment of tropical illness.

International Association for Medical Assistance to Travelers
417 Center Street
Lewiston
NY 14092
Tel: **716-754 4883**
http://www.sentex.net/~iamat
Non-profit organisation dedicated to the gathering and dissemination of health and sanitary information world-wide. Publishes a directory of English-speaking medical centres world-wide and many leaflets on world climates, immunisation, malaria and other health risks world-wide.
also at
40 Regal Road
Guelph, Ontario
N1K 1B5
Canada
Tel: **519-836 0102**

Liverpool School of Tropical Medicine
Pembroke Place
Liverpool L3 5QA
Tel: **0151-708 9393**
Clinic open 1pm-4pm Mon-Fri, no appointments necessary.
Pre-recorded travel health, vaccination and malaria advice on 0891-172111 - 50p per minute.
http://www.liv.ac.uk/lstm/tra velmed.html.
Regular immunisation and post-travel clinic with a range of travellers' health supplies. An international centre of expertise and research on venoms and snake bites, and investigation and management of tropical diseases.

Malaria Reference Laboratory
Tel: **0171-636 7921/8636**
Advice on malaria prophylaxis and prevention.

Biting Insects and How to Avoid Getting Bitten Advice Line
Tel: **0891-600 270**
Calls cost 50p per minute.

MASTA
London School of Hygiene and Tropical Medicine
Keppel Street
London WC1E 7BR
Tel: **0171-631 4408**
Health Brief: **0891-224 100**
Markets a wide range of products. For detailed advice on all health requirements for your intended destination(s), ring the Health Brief line; calls typically take 3-4 minutes and following this your health brief

arrives by first class post (covered by the cost of the call).

Ross Institute Malaria Advisory Service
London School of Hygiene and Tropical Medicine
Keppel Street
London WC1E 7HT
Tel: **0171-636 7921**
24-hour taped advice.

Travellers' Healthline
Tel: **0891-224 100**
This is a regularly updated advice line (with inter-active technology) for travellers seeking information about vaccinations etc.

UDS Department of Health and Human Services
Public Health Service
Centers for Disease Control,
Center for Prevention Service
Division of Quarantine
101 Marietta Street, Rm 1515
Atlanta
GA 30323
Tel: **404-331 2442**

West London Designated Vaccination Centre
53 Great Cumberland Place
London W1H 7HL
Tel: **0171-262 6456**
Open 8.45am-5pm Mon-Fri, no appointment necessary.

WEXAS Healthline
Tel: **0839 337730** (49p per minute)
WEXAS members' exclusive traveller's health information service: see the Directory of Membership Services.

HIV/AIDS INFORMATION

National AIDS Helpline
Tel: 0800 567 123
24-hour free helpline providing advice on all aspects of HIV infection.

Positive Discounts
PO Box 347
Twickenham
TW1 2SN
Tel: **0181-891 2561**
http://www.positive-discounts.org.uk
Travel insurance whether or not you are HIV+.

Terence Higgins Trust
Tel: **0171-242 1010**
Confidential phoneline for detailed information about travel restrictions, insurance etc. for HIV+ individuals.

BRITISH AIRWAYS TRAVEL CLINICS

These clinics provide a comprehensive vaccination and travellers' health information service to anyone, regardless of whether or not they travel by British Airways. Please ring first to make an appointment.

A useful benefit has been negotiated for WEXAS members, who are entitled to a discount of £5, if they spend more than £10, at all the following clinics:

CENTRAL LONDON:

City of London EC2
0171-606 2977

Fulham SW6
0171-731 7354

Hampstead NW3
0171-433 1331

Victoria Station SW1
0171-233 6661

Regent Street W1
0171-439 9584

Tottenham Court Road W1
0171-637 9899

Wimbledon SW19
0181-944 0088

Wimpole Street W1
0171-486 3665

SOUTH EAST ENGLAND

Brighton
01273-606636

Cambridge
01223-313969

Gatwick Airport
01293-666255

Harrow
0181-861 1181

Heathrow Airport
0181-562 5825

Hemel Hempstead
01442-236733

Purley
0181-763 1372

Reading
0118-957 5101

Stoke Poges (Bucks)
01753-662243

Shenfield (Essex)
01277-200169

Tonbridge (Kent)
01732-771001

SOUTH WEST ENGLAND

Bristol
0117-975 5500

Plymouth
01752-205556

WALES

Cardiff
01222-811425

CENTRAL ENGLAND

Birmingham
0121-523 2522

Milton Keynes
01908-211035

Newcastle-under-Lyme
01782-713173

Nottingham
0115-962 6148

Stratford-upon-Avon
01789-268249

NORTH AND NORTH EAST ENGLAND

Chester
01244-377844

Manchester
0161-832 3019

Newcastle-upon-Tyne
0191-230 3721

York
01904-784484

SCOTLAND

Aberdeen - 01224-624669

Edinburgh - 0131-336 3038

EMERGENCY TRAVEL MEDICAL KIT SUPPLIERS

Homeway Ltd
Fighting Cocks
West Amesbury
Salisbury
Wilts SP4 7BH
Tel: **01980-626361**
Provides a Travel with Care package and also sells sterile medical packs.

Dr Jones and Partners
Charlotte Keel Health Centre
Seymour Road
Easton
Bristol BS5 0UA
Tel: **0117-951 2244**
Travel medical kits.

Medical Advisory Services for Travellers (MASTA)
London School of Hygiene and Tropical Medicine
Keppel Street
London WC1
Tel: **0171-631 4408**
MASTA has helped to design the 'Travel-Well' personal water purifiers. It removes particulate matter, bacteria, protozoa and viruses from contaminated water. The Trekker Travel Well costs £24.95 and the Pocket Travel Well costs £9.95. They also sell Sterile Medical Equipment Packs and Emergency Dental Packs.

DIRECTORY

Nomad
3-4 Wellington Terrace
Turnpike Lane
Hornsey
London N8 0PX
Tel: **0181-889 7014**
or
4 Potters Road
New Barnet
Hertfordshire
EN5 5HW
Tel: **0181-441 7208**
Full medical centre, immunisation and pharmacy. Wide range of not only medical equipment, but also clothing and mosquito nets. Mail order.

Oasis
High Street
Stoke Ferry
King's Lynn
Norfolk
PE33 9SP
Tel: **01366-500466**
Not only sells mosquito nets, but will also send a free malaria advice sheet, also can provide sterile medical kits.

Safety and First Aid (SAFA)
59 Hill Street
Liverpool L8 5SB
Tel: **0151-708 0397**
As well as general medical kits also provide Aids and Hepatitis B prevention kits.

MAJOR HOSPITALS WORLD-WIDE

This list is not comprehensive, but is intended as an initial guide, listing one important hospital in capital cities world-wide.

Albania
ABC Clinic (British Clinic),
Rruga Ludovik Shllaku,
Tirana
Tel: **42-27707 / 29752**

Algeria
Hospital Mustapha,
Place du 1er Mai,
Algiers
Tel: **2-67 33 33**

Andorra
Hospital Nostra Senyora de Meritxell,
13 Av Fiter I Rossell,
Escalades-Engordany
Tel: **871 000**

Anguilla
Princess Alexandra Hospital,
Stoney Ground,
Anguilla BW1
Tel: **809-497 2552**

Antigua and Barbuda
Holberton Hospital,
Queen Elizabeth Highway,
St. John's
Tel: **462 0251/4**

Argentina
Hospital general de Agudos,
Cerviño 3356,
Buenos Aires
Tel: **1-801 0027/801 0412**

Armenia
Republican Clinical
Hospital,
6 Margarian Street,
Achapniak,
Yerevan
Tel: **2-34 50 83**

Australia:
(NSW)
Royal Prince Albert
Hospital,
Missenden Road,
Camerdown 2050,
Sydney
Tel: **2-516 6111**

(Northern Territory)
Royal Darwin
Hospital,
Rocklands Drive,
Casuarina
Tel: **89-228 888**

(Queensland)
Royal Brisbane
Hospital,
Herston Road,
Herston,
Brisbane
Tel: **7-3253 8111/
8222**

(South Australia)
Royal Adelaide
Hospital,
North Terrace,
Adelaide
Tel: **8-223 0230**

(Tasmania)
Royal Hobart
Hospital,
Liverpool Street,
Hobart
Tel: **2-388 308**

(Victoria)
Central Wellington
Health Service,

Guthridge Parade,
Sale 3850
Tel: **51-44 41 11**

(Western Australia)
Royal Perth Hospital,
Wellington Street,
Perth WA6000
Tel: **9-224 2244**

Austria
Allgemeines
Krankenhaus,
18-20 Waehringer
Guertal,
Vienna A-1090
Tel: **1-402 0660**

Azerbaijan
Semashko Clinical
Hospital No. 1,
1M Kasimova Street,
Baku
Tel: **12-95 49 04**

Bahamas
Princess Margaret
Hospital,
Shirley Street and
Elizabeth Avenue,
Nassau
Tel: **322 2861**

Bahrain
International Hospital
of Bahrain,
PO Box 1084,
Manama
Tel: **591 666**

Bangladesh
Dhaka Medical
College Hospital,
Tel: **2-31 82 02**

Barbados
Queen Elizabeth
Hospital,
Martindales Road,

St. Michael
Tel: **436 6450**

Belarus
Minsk Clinic No. 10,
73 Uborevich Street,
Minsk
Tel: **172-419 811**

Belgium
Clinique Univeritaire
St Luc,
Avenue Hippocrate 10
Brussels 1200
Tel: **2-555 3111**

Belize
Karl Heusner
Memorial Hospital,
Princess Margaret
Drive,
Belize City
Tel: **2-31548**

Benin
Centre Hospitalier
Départemental de
l'Ouémé,
Porto Novo
Tel: **21 32 29**

Bermuda
King Edward VII
Memorial Hospital,
Hamilton HM DX
Tel: **236 2345**

Bhutan
Jigme Dorji
Wamgchuk National
Referral Hospital,
Thimphu
Tel: **2-22496/7**

Bolivia
Hospital General,
Avenida Saavedra
2245,
La Paz ⇨

DIRECTORY

Tel: **2-367 711**

Botswana
Princess Marina
Hospital,
Gaborone
Tel: **353 221**

Brazil
Hospital de Base do
Distrito Federal,
Area Especial SMHS,
Brasilia
Tel: **61-325 5050**

Brunei
Raja Isteri Pengiran
Anak Saleha Hospital
(RIPAS),
Bandar Seri Begawan
Tel: **2-242424**

Bulgaria
Medical University
Hospital "Sveta
Anna",
Sofia
Tel: **2-75 51 24**

Burkina Faso
Clinique Notre Dame
de la Paix,
BP5666,
Tanghin secteur 24,
Ouagadougou
Tel: **36 26 40**

Burundi
Clinique Prince Louis
Rwagasore,
Bujumbura
Tel: **2-223 881/2**

Cambodia
European Medical
Clinic,
195a Norodom Blvd,
Phnom Penh
Tel: **23-91200**

Cameroon
Centre Médico-Social
(Coopération
Française),
Yaoundé
Tel: **22/23-230 139**

Central African Republic
Hôpital de l'Amitie,
Ave de
l'Independance,
Bangui
Tel: **615 700**

Chad
Hôpital Central
N'Djaména Capitol,
BP77
Tel: **515 309 / 515 336**

Chile
Hospital Jose Joaquin
Aguirre,
999 Santos Dumont,
Santiago
Tel: **2-737 3031**

China
Beijing Hospital,
1 Dahua Road,
Dongdan,
Beijing 100730
Tel: **10-513 2266**

Colombia
San Juan de dios,
carrera 10,
Calle de la Sur,
Santa Fe de Bogotá
Tel: **1-233 4044**

Congo
Centra Hospitalier et
Universitaire,
de Brazzaville,
BP32
Tel: **82 88 10/ 82 23 65**

Costa Rica
Hospital México,
San José
Tel: **232 6122**

Côte d'Ivoire
Centre Hospitalier et
Universitaire de
Cocody,
Yamoussoukro
Tel: **44 91 00/ 44 90 38**

Croatia
KBC Zagreb,
Salata 2,
Tel: **1-273457**

Cuba
Civa Garcia
International Clinic,
Havana
Tel: **7-332 605**

Cyprus
Lefkosia General
Hospital,
Nicosia
Tel: **2-451 111**

Czech Republic
Nemocnice na
Homolce,
2 Roentgenove,
151 19 Prague 5
Tel: **2-52921111**

Denmark
Rogshospitalet,
Copenhagen Ø,
DK-2100
Tel: **45-35 45 35 45**

Djibouti
Hôpital Peltier,
Djibouti
Tel: **35 27 12**

Dominica
Princess Margaret
Hospital,
Goodwill,
Roseau
Tel: **448 2231**

**Dominican
Republic**
Hospital Dr Dario
Contreras,
Santo Domingo,
Tel: **596 3686 /
596 7231**

Ecuador
Hospital
Metropolitano,
Ave Mariana Jesús y
Occidental,
Quito
Tel: **2-431 520
/439 030**

Egypt
3 Syria Street,
Mohessien,
Cairo
Tel: **2-3029091/5**

El Salvador
Hospital de Ninos
Benjamin Bloom,
25 Av Norte Final,
San Salvador
Tel: **225 4692**

Eritrea
Mekane Hiwot
Hospital,
Asmara
Tel: **1-127762**

Estonia
Mustamae Haigla,
19 Sutiste Tee
Tallinn EE0034
Tel: **7-428 211**

Ethiopia
Black Lion Hospital,
Addis Ababa
Tel: **1-511211**

Fiji
Colonial War
Memorial Hospital,
Suva
Tel: **679-321 066**

Finland
Helsinki University
Central Hospital,
Stenbackinpratu 9,
Helsinki
Tel: **0-4711**

France
Cochin Hospital,
27 rue du Faubourg St
Jacques,
Paris
Tel: **1-42 34 12 12**

French Guiana
Centre Hospitalier
Général de Cayenne,
Ave des Flamboyants,
Cayenne
Tel: **39 50 50**

Gabon
Centre Hospitalier de
Libreville,
BP 50
Tel: **76 36 18**

Gambia
Royal Victoria
Hospital,
Banjul
Tel: **228 223**

Georgia
Treatment and
Diagnostic Centre,
5 I Chavchavdze Ave,
Tbilisi
Tel: **32-23 04 92**

Germany
Krankenhauser
Klinikum Buch,
50 Wiltberghstr,
Berlin 13125
Tel: **30-94010**

Ghana
Ridge Hospital,
Castle Road,
Accra
Tel: **21-775341**

Greece
Regional General
Hospital
Evangelismos,
Tpsilantou 45,
Athens
Tel: **1-722 0101/722
1501**

Grenada
General Hospital,
St George's
Tel: **440 2051**

Guatemala
Hospital Centro
Medico,
6a Av 3-47,
Zona 10,
Guatemala City
Tel: **2-323 555/
342 157**

Guinea Republic
CHU Donka,
BP 234,
Conakry
Tel: **44 19 33/
44 46 86**

Guinea-Bissau
Simão Mendes
National Hospital,
Bissau
Tel: **212 861**

DIRECTORY

Guyana
Georgetown Hospital,
New Market Street,
Georgetown
Tel: **2-56900**

Haiti
Hôpital Saint François
de Sales,
rue Chareron,
Port-au-Prince
Tel: **22 5033**

Hong Kong
Queen Elizabeth
Hospital,
30 Gascoigne Road,
Kowloon
Tel: **2958 8888**

Hungary
Szent János Kórház,
1 Diósárok Ucta,
Budapest 1125
Tel: **1-156 1122/
1410**

Iceland
Landspítalinn,
v/Hringbraut,
Reykjavík 101
Tel: **560 1000**

India
Appollo Hospital,
Saritarihar,
Delhi Maghura Road,
New Delhi
Tel: **11-6925858**

Indonesia
Cipto Mangun
Kusuma Hospital,
Diponogoro 71,
Jakarta Central
Tel: **21-566 8284**

Iran
Imam Khomeini
Hospital,
End of Kesharvarz
Blvd,
Tehran
Tel: **21-938 081**

Iraq
WHO representative
Dr Habib Rejab,
c/o UNDP Office,
PO Box 2048,
Baghdad
Tel: **1-718 0875**

Ireland
Beaumont Hospital,
Beaumont Road,
Dublin 9
Tel: **1-837 7755**

Israel
Kiryah Hadassah,
Jerusalem
Tel: **2-777111**

Italy
Ospedale Agostino
Gemelli,
8 Largo Gemelli,
Rome 00168
Tel: **6-30151**

Jamaica
University of West
Indies,
Mona,
Kingston 7
Tel: **927 1620**

Japan
International Clinic,
5-9 Azabudai 1-
chrome,
Minato-ku,
Tokyo
Tel: **3-582 2646**

Jordan
Al Basheer Hospital,
Amman
Tel: **6-775111**

Kazakhstan
Adult Medical Care
Diagnostic Centre,
57 Auezova Street,
Almaty
Tel: **3272-42 29 79**

Kenya
Kenyatta National
Hospital,
Nairobi
Tel: **2-726 300**

Korea (North)
Korean Red Cross
General Hospital,
Pyongyang

Korea (South)
Seoul National
University Hospital,
28 Yon-gon-dong,
Chongno-gu
Tel: **2-760 2114**

Kuwait
Al Amiri Hospital,
Safat 13041,
Kuwait City
Tel: **2451442**

Kyrgystan
Rep. Clinical Hospital
No 1,
Togolok Moldo Street
1,
Bishkek 720011
Tel: **3312-223424**

Laos
International Clinic,
Fangum Road,
Vientiane
Tel: **21-214 022**

Latvia
Latvian Medical
Academy,
13 Pilsonu,
Riga LV 1002
Tel: **2-611 198**

Lebanon
Beirut General
Hospital,
Tel: **1-850213/4**

Lesotho
Queen Elizabeth II
Hospital,
PO Box 122,
Maseru
Tel: **322501**

Libya
El Khadra Hospital,
Tripoli
Tel: **21-903301**

Lithuania
Vilnius University
Emergency Hospital,
Siltnamiu 29,
Vilnius
Tel: **2-269 069/140**

Luxembourg
Clinique d'Eich,
78 rue d'Eich,
Luxembourg-Ville
Tel: **43 77 71**

Macau
Hospital Kiang Wu,
Rua de Kiang
Tel: **37 13 33**

Macedonia
Clinical Centre of the
Rep. of Macedonia,
17 Vodnjanska Street,
Skopje
Tel: **91-114 244**

Madagascar
Hôpital Général de
Befelatanana,
Mahamasina,
Antananarivo 101
Tel: **2-22384**

Malawi
Kamuzu Central
Hospital,
Lilongwe
Tel: **721 555**

Malaysia
General Hospital,
Jalan Pahang,
Kuala Lumpur 50586
Tel: **3-292 1044**

Maldives
Indira Gandhi
Memorial Hospital,
Malé
Tel: **316 647**

Mali
French Medical
Centre,
Bamako
Tel: **225071**

Malta
St. Luke's Hospital,
Guardamangia
Tel: **241 251/
234 101/247 860**

Mauritania
Centre Hospitalier
National,
Nouakchott
Tel: **2-52135**

Mauritius
Dr A Jeetoo Hospital,
Volcy Pougnet Street,
Port Louis
Tel: **2123201**

Mexico
Hospital General,
Andador 5,
entre Calle 12 y Calle
13,
Cancún,
QR
Tel: **98-842666**

Moldova
Republican Clinical
Hospital,
29 Strada N
Testemitanu,
Chisinău
Tel: **2-72 85 85**

Mongolia
National Medical
Institute,
Ard Augushin Street,
Ulan Bator
Tel: **1-361155**

Morocco
Clinique Agdal,
6 Place Talha,
Ave Ibn Sina,
Agdal,
Rabat
Tel: **7-770100/
675030**

Myanmar
AEA International
Clinic,
Nawarat Arcade,
257 Insein Road,
Hlaing Township
11052,
Yangon

Namibia
Medicity Windhoek,
Heliodoor Street,
Eros Park,
Windhoek
Tel: **61-222687**

DIRECTORY

Nepal
Anandaban Hospital,
Kathmandu
Tel: **1-290545**

The Netherlands
Academisch Medisch
Centrum,
Meibergdreef 9,
Amsterdam 1105 AZ
Tel: **20-5669111**

New Zealand
Auckland Hospital,
Park Road,
Grafton
Tel: **9-379 7440**

Nicaragua
La Mascota,
Managua,
Tel: **2-289 7700**

Niger
Hôpital National de
Niamey,
BP 238,
Niamey
Tel: **72 22 53/
72 28 55/72 25 21**

Nigeria
St Nicholas Hospital,
57 Campbell Street,
Lagos
Tel: **1-2600070-9**

Norway
Rikshospitalet,
32 Pilestredet,
Oslo 0027
Tel: **22-86 70 10**

Oman
The Royal Hospital,
PO Box 1331,
Muscat 111,
Tel: **590491**

Pakistan
Federal Government
Services Hospital,
Islamabad
Tel: **51-218300/
859511-19**

Panama
Hospital Santo
Tomás,
Ave 1,
Panamá 1,
Tel: **227 4075**

**Papua New
Guinea**
Port Moresby General
Hospital,
Boroko 111
Tel: **3248200**

Paraguay
Sanatorio Migone
Battilana,
Eligio Ayala 1293,
Asunción
Tel: **021-498200**

Peru
Hospital de
Emergencia
"Casimiru Ulloa",
Ave Republica de
Panama,
Lima
Tel: **1-445 5096**

Philippines
St Luke's Medical
Center,
279 E Rodriquez
Senior Blvd,
Manilla
Tel: **2-799661**

Poland
Centralny Szpital
Kliniczny,
1A Banacha Street,

Warsaw 02-097
Tel: **22-6583516**

Portugal
Hospital Santa Maria,
Avenida Prof. Egas
Moniz,
Lisbon 1600
Tel: **1-7975171**

Puerto Rico
University District
Hospital,
Puerto Rico Medical
Center,
San Juan
Tel: **754 3700/
754 3600**

Qatar
Hamad General
Hospital,
PO Box 3050,
Doha
Tel: **394444**

Romania
The Emergency
Hospital,
10 Sos Berceni,
Sector 4,
Bucharest
Tel: **1-6836895**

Russia
American Medical
Center,
Bldg No. 10,
2nd Tverskoy-
Yamskoy Per,
Moscow
Tel: **095-956 33 66**

Rwanda
CHK (Centre
Hospitalier de Kigali),
Ave de l'Hopital,
Kigali
Tel: **75555**

Saudi Arabia
Riyadh Central
Hospital,
Riyadh 11196
Tel: **1-435 5555**

Senegal
Hôpital Principal,
Ave Nelson Mandela,
Dakar
Tel: **232 741**

Seychelles
Victoria Hospital,
PO Box 52,
Victoria,
Mahé
Tel: **388 000**

Sierra Leone
Connaught Hospital,
1 Johnston Street,
Freetown
Tel: **22-222 962**

Singapore
Singapore General
Hospital,
Outram Road,
Singapore
Tel: **2223322**

Slovak Republic
Berer 3 Hospital,
5 Limbová,
Bratislava
Tel: **7-374 503**

Slovenia
Klinicni Center
Ljubljana,
7 Zaloska,
Ljublijana
Tel: **61-1313113**

Solomon Islands
Central Hospital,
Honiara
Tel: **23 600**

Somalia
Benadir Hospital,
Mogadishu

South Africa
Entabeni Hospital,
PO Box 2230,
Durban 4000
Tel: **31-811344**

Spain
Hospital 12 de
Octubre,
Carretera de
Andalucia,
Madrid 4-28041
Tel: **1-469 7600/
460 4000**

Sri Lanka
National Hospital,
Columbo
Tel: **1-691111/ 698443**

Sudan
Khartoum Teaching
Hospital,
PO Box 102,
Khartoum
Tel: **11-770208**

Suriname
Academisch
Ziekenhuis,
PO Box 389,
Flustraat,
Paramaribo
Tel: **498552**

Swaziland
Mbabane Government
Hospital,
PO Box 8,
Mbabane
Tel: **42111**

Sweden
Karolinsko Sjukhuset,
171 76 Stockholm

Tel: **8-729 2000**

Switzerland
Inselspital,
Freiburg Strasse 18,
Bern 3010
Tel: **31-6322802**

Tahiti
Hôpital Mamao,
Papeete
Tel: **466262**

Taiwan
Cathay General
Hospital,
280 Jen Ai Road,
Section 4,
Taipei
Tel: **2-7082121**

Tajikistan
Karaboloev Medical
Centre,
59 Samoni,
Dushanbe
Tel: **3772-361510**

Tanzania
Muhimbil Medical
Centre,
PO Box 65000,
Dar es Salaam
Tel: **51-26211**

Thailand
Bangkok General
Hospital,
2 Soi Soonvichai 7,
Bangkok
Tel: **2-318 0066**

Togo
Centre Hospalier
Universitaire,
PO Box 57,
Tokoin,
Lomé
Tel: **212501/215072/**

DIRECTORY

254739

Trinidad and Tobago

Port of Spain General Hospital,
Charlotte Street,
Tel: **632 951**

Tunisia

Hôpital Charles Nicole,
Blvd Bab Benat,
Tunis
Tel: **1-663 000/949**

Turkey

University of Hacettepe Hospital,
Hacettepe,
Ankara
Tel: **312-3103545**

Turkmenistan

The Central Clinical Hospital,
UI Gorgoli,
Pirigova NI,
Ashgabat
Tel: **3632-253243**

Uganda

Mulago Hospital,
PO Box 7051,
Kampala
Tel: **41-541250**

Ukraine

Ukrainian Medical Service,
16 Olzhicha Street,
Kiev 86
Tel: **44-440 63 44**

United Arab Emirates

Al Jazira Hospital,
PO Box 2427,
Abu Dhabi
Tel: **2-214800**

Uruguay

British Hospital,
2420 Ave Italia,
Montevideo
Tel: **2-471020**

Uzbekistan

International Medical Clinic,
4 Taras Shevchenko Street,
Tashkent
Tel: **3712-560606**

Venezuela

Hospital Clinico Universitario,
Ciudad Universitaria,
Caracas
Tel: **2-6627540**

Vietnam

Bach Mai Medical Centre,
Foreigner Admittance,
Phuong Mai Street,
Hanoi
Tel: **4-8522089**

Yemen

Al Thawra Hospital,
Sana'a
Tel: **1-246972**

Yugoslavia

Klinicki Centar Beograd,
2 Pasterova,
Belgrade 11000
Tel: **11-662 755/ 661 122**

Zaïre (DRC)

Zaïre American Clinic
1054 Ave Batétéla
Kinshasa
Tel: **12-50929**

Zambia

University Teaching Hospital,
Lusaka
Tel: **1-253955**

Zimbabwe

Parirenyatwa Hospital,
PO Box CY 198,
Causeway,
Harare
Tel: **4-794411**

Further information: World Travel Health Guide (Columbus Press)

COUNTRY BY COUNTRY MALARIA RISK AND VACCINATION GUIDE

The following is a country by country list of recommended immunisations, which may alter according to local conditions and times of year. Refer to your local travel clinic for the latest advice. Long term travellers should also consider the following additional vaccines: hepatitis B, BCG, rabies, Japanese encephalitis (if travelling in Asia). See *Vaccines* in Chapter 1.

Key	* immunisation against yellow fever essential (i.e. documentary proof of immunisation may be required) if arriving from an infected area (this will not apply if you are coming from the UK).
	** immunisation essential entry requirement.
	ʳ yellow fever immunisation recommended.
	^ Malaria present in certain areas of the country.
	No immunisations are recommended for the countries that are not listed here.

Afghanistan	Hep. A, Polio, Typhoid, Malaria, Y. Fever*
Albania	Hep. A, Polio, Typhoid, Y. Fever*
Algeria	Hep. A, Polio, Typhoid, Y. Fever*
Angola	Hep. A, Polio, Typhoid, Malaria, Y. Fever*ʳ
Anguilla	Hep. A, Polio, Typhoid, Y. Fever*
Antigua and Barbuda	Hep. A, Polio, Typhoid, Y. Fever*
Argentina	Hep. A, Polio, Typhoid, Malaria^
Armenia	Hep. A, Polio, Typhoid
Aruba	Y. Fever*
Australia	Y. Fever*
Azerbaijan	Hep. A, Polio, Typhoid, Malaria^, Diphtheria
Bahamas	Hep. A, Polio, Typhoid, Y. Fever*
Bahrain	Hep. A, Polio, Typhoid
Bali	Hep. A, Polio, Typhoid, Y. Fever*
Bangladesh	Hep. A, Polio, Typhoid, Malaria, Y. Fever*
Barbados	Hep. A, Polio, Typhoid, Y. Fever*
Belarus	Hep. A, Polio, Typhoid, Diphtheria
Belize	Hep. A, Polio, Typhoid, Malaria, Y. Fever*
Benin	Hep. A, Polio, Typhoid, Malaria, Y. Fever**, Meningitis
Bhutan	Hep. A, Polio, Typhoid, Malaria^, Y. Fever*, Meningitis

DIRECTORY

Bolivia	Hep. A, Polio, Typhoid, Malaria, Y. Fever*ʳ
Bonaire	Hep. A, Polio, Typhoid
Bosnia Herzegovina	Hep. A, Polio, Typhoid
Botswana	Hep. A, Polio, Typhoid, Malaria^
Brazil	Hep. A, Polio, Typhoid, Malaria, Y. Fever*ʳ
Brunei	Hep. A, Polio, Typhoid, Y. Fever*
Bulgaria	Hep. A, Polio, Typhoid
Burkina Faso	Hep. A, Polio, Typhoid, Malaria, Y. Fever**, Meningitis
Burma (Myanmar)	Hep. A, Polio, Typhoid, Malaria, Y. Fever*
Burundi	Hep. A, Polio, Typhoid, Malaria, Y. Fever*, Meningitis
Cambodia	Hep. A, Polio, Typhoid, Malaria, Y. Fever*
Cameroon	Hep. A, Polio, Typhoid, Malaria, Y. Fever**, Meningitis
Cape Verde	Hep. A, Polio, Typhoid, Malaria^, Y. Fever*
Cayman Islands	Hep. A, Polio, Typhoid
Central African Rep.	Hep. A, Polio, Typhoid, Malaria, Y. Fever**, Meningitis
Chad	Hep. A, Polio, Typhoid, Malaria, Y. Feverʳ, Meningitis
Chile	Hep. A, Polio, Typhoid
China	Hep. A, Polio, Typhoid, Malaria^, Y. Fever*
Colombia	Hep. A, Polio, Typhoid, Malaria, Y. Feverʳ
Comoros	Hep. A, Polio, Typhoid, Malaria
Congo	Hep. A, Polio, Typhoid, Malaria, Y. Fever**
Cook Islands	Hep. A, Polio, Typhoid
Costa Rica	Hep. A, Polio, Typhoid, Malaria
Côte d' Ivoire	Hep. A, Polio, Typhoid, Malaria, Y. Fever**, Meningitis
Croatia	Hep. A, Polio, Typhoid
Cuba	Hep. A, Polio, Typhoid
Curaçao	Hep. A, Polio, Typhoid
Czech Republic	Hep. A, Polio, Typhoid
Djibouti	Hep. A, Polio, Typhoid, Malaria, Y. Fever*, Meningitis
Dominica	Hep. A, Polio, Typhoid, Y. Fever*
Dominican Republic	Hep. A, Polio, Typhoid, Malaria
Ecuador	Hep. A, Polio, Typhoid, Malaria, Y. Fever*ʳ
Egypt	Hep. A, Polio, Typhoid, Malaria^, Y. Fever*
El Salvador	Hep. A, Polio, Typhoid, Malaria, Y. Fever*
Equatorial Guinea	Hep. A, Polio, Typhoid, Malaria, Y. Fever*ʳ
Eritrea	Hep. A, Polio, Typhoid, Malaria^, Y. Fever*

Estonia	Hep. A, Polio, Typhoid, Diphtheria
Ethiopia	Hep. A, Polio, Typhoid, Malaria, Y. Fever*[r], Meningitis
Falkland Islands	Hep. A, Polio, Typhoid
Fiji	Hep. A, Polio, Typhoid, Y. Fever*
French Guiana	Hep. A, Polio, Typhoid, Malaria, Y. Fever**
Gabon	Hep. A, Polio, Typhoid, Malaria, Y. Fever**
The Gambia	Hep. A, Polio, Typhoid, Malaria, Y. Fever*[r], Meningitis
Georgia	Hep. A, Polio, Typhoid, Diphtheria
Ghana	Hep. A, Polio, Typhoid, Malaria, Y. Fever**, Meningitis
Greece	Y. Fever*
Grenada	Hep. A, Polio, Typhoid, Y. Fever*
Guadeloupe	Hep. A, Polio, Typhoid, Y. Fever*
Guam	Hep. A, Polio, Typhoid
Guatemala	Hep. A, Polio, Typhoid, Malaria, Y. Fever*
Guinea Republic	Hep. A, Polio, Typhoid, Malaria, Y. Fever*[r], Meningitis
Guinea-Bissau	Hep. A, Polio, Typhoid, Malaria, Y. Fever*[r], Meningitis
Guyana	Hep. A, Polio, Typhoid, Malaria, Y. Fever*[r]
Haiti	Hep. A, Polio, Typhoid, Malaria, Y. Fever*
Honduras	Hep. A, Polio, Typhoid, Malaria, Y. Fever*
Hong Kong	Hep. A, Polio, Typhoid
India	Hep. A, Polio, Typhoid, Malaria, Y. Fever*, Meningitis
Indonesia	Hep. A, Polio, Typhoid, Malaria^, Y. Fever*
Iran	Hep. A, Polio, Typhoid, Malaria
Iraq	Hep. A, Polio, Typhoid, Malaria, Y. Fever*
Israel	Hep. A, Polio, Typhoid
Jamaica	Hep. A, Polio, Typhoid, Y. Fever*
Japan	Hep. A, Polio, Typhoid
Jordan	Hep. A, Polio, Typhoid, Y. Fever*
Kazakhstan	Hep. A, Polio, Typhoid, Y. Fever*, Diphtheria
Kenya	Hep. A, Polio, Typhoid, Malaria, Y. Fever*[r], Meningitis
Kiribati	Hep. A, Polio, Typhoid, Y. Fever*
Korea (Dem. Rep)	Hep. A, Polio, Typhoid
Korea (South)	Hep. A, Polio, Typhoid
Kuwait	Hep. A, Polio, Typhoid
Kyrgyzstan	Hep. A, Polio, Typhoid, Diphtheria
Laos	Hep. A, Polio, Typhoid, Malaria, Y. Fever*

Latvia	Hep. A, Polio, Typhoid, Diphtheria
Lebanon	Hep. A, Polio, Typhoid, Y. Fever*
Lesotho	Hep. A, Polio, Typhoid, Y. Fever*
Liberia	Hep. A, Polio, Typhoid, Malaria, Y. Fever**, Meningitis
Libya	Hep. A, Polio, Typhoid, Y. Fever*
Lithuania	Hep. A, Polio, Typhoid, Diphtheria
Macau	Hep. A, Polio, Typhoid
Macedonia	Hep. A, Polio, Typhoid
Madagascar	Hep. A, Polio, Typhoid, Malaria, Y. Fever*
Madeira	Y. Fever*
Malawi	Hep. A, Polio, Typhoid, Malaria, Y. Fever*, Meningitis
Malaysia	Hep. A, Polio, Typhoid, Malaria^, Y. Fever*
Maldives	Hep. A, Polio, Typhoid, Y. Fever*
Mali	Hep. A, Polio, Typhoid, Malaria, Y. Fever**, Meningitis
Malta	Y. Fever*
Martinique	Hep. A, Polio, Typhoid, Y. Fever*
Mauritania	Hep. A, Polio, Typhoid, Malaria, Y. Fever**
Mauritius	Hep. A, Polio, Typhoid, Y. Fever*
Mexico	Hep. A, Polio, Typhoid, Malaria, Y. Fever*
Moldova	Hep. A, Polio, Typhoid, Diphtheria
Mongolia	Hep. A, Polio, Typhoid
Monserrat	Hep. A, Polio, Typhoid
Morocco	Hep. A, Polio, Typhoid
Mozambique	Hep. A, Polio, Typhoid, Malaria, Y. Fever*, Meningitis
Namibia	Hep. A, Polio, Typhoid, Malaria, Y. Fever*
Nauru	Hep. A, Polio, Typhoid, Y. Fever*
Nepal	Hep. A, Polio, Typhoid, Malaria, Y. Fever*, Meningitis
Netherlands Antilles	Hep. A, Polio, Typhoid, Y. Fever*
New Caledonia	Hep. A, Polio, Typhoid, Y. Fever*
Nicarugua	Hep. A, Polio, Typhoid, Malaria, Y. Fever*
Niger	Hep. A, Polio, Typhoid, Malaria, Y. Fever**, Meningitis
Nigeria	Hep. A, Polio, Typhoid, Malaria, Y. Fever*', Meningitis
Niue	Hep. A, Polio, Typhoid, Y. Fever*
Oman	Hep. A, Polio, Typhoid, Malaria, Y. Fever*
Pakistan	Hep. A, Polio, Typhoid, Malaria, Y. Fever*, Meningitis
Panama	Hep. A, Polio, Typhoid, Malaria, Y. Fever*',

Papua New Guinea	Hep. A, Polio, Typhoid, Malaria, Y. Fever*
Paraguay	Hep. A, Polio, Typhoid, Malaria, Y. Fever*
Peru	Hep. A, Polio, Typhoid, Malaria, Y. Fever*ʳ
Philippines	Hep. A, Polio, Typhoid, Malaria^, Y. Fever*
Pitcairn Island	Hep. A, Polio, Typhoid, Y. Fever*
Portugal	Y. Fever *
Polynesia	Hep. A, Polio, Typhoid, Y. Fever*
Puerto Rico	Hep. A, Polio, Typhoid
Qatar	Hep. A, Polio, Typhoid
Réunion	Hep. A, Polio, Typhoid, Y. Fever*
Romania	Hep. A, Polio, Typhoid
Russian Federation	Hep. A, Polio, Typhoid, Diphtheria
Rwanda	Hep. A, Polio, Typhoid, Malaria, Y. Fever**, Meningitis
Saba	Hep. A, Polio, Typhoid, Y. Fever*
St. Eustatius	Hep. A, Polio, Typhoid, Y. Fever*
St. Helena	Hep. A, Polio, Typhoid
St Kitts and Nevis	Hep. A, Polio, Typhoid, Y. Fever*
St. Lucia	Hep. A, Polio, Typhoid, Y. Fever*
St. Maarten	Hep. A, Polio, Typhoid, Y. Fever*
St. Vincent and Gren.	Hep. A, Polio, Typhoid, Y. Fever*
Samoa (Western)	Hep. A, Polio, Typhoid, Y. Fever*
São Tomé and Prin.	Hep. A, Polio, Typhoid, Malaria, Y. Fever**
Saudi Arabia	Hep. A, Polio, Typhoid, Malaria, Y. Fever*, Meningitis
Senegal	Hep. A, Polio, Typhoid, Malaria, Y. Fever*ʳ, Meningitis
Seychelles	Hep. A, Polio, Typhoid, Y. Fever*
Sierra Leone	Hep. A, Polio, Typhoid, Malaria, Y. Fever*ʳ, Meningitis
Singapore	Hep. A, Polio, Typhoid, Y. Fever*
Slovak Republic	Hep. A, Polio, Typhoid
Slovenia	Hep. A, Polio, Typhoid
Solomon Islands	Hep. A, Polio, Typhoid, Malaria, Y. Fever*
Somalia	Hep. A, Polio, Typhoid, Malaria, Y. Fever*ʳ, Meningitis
South Africa	Hep. A, Polio, Typhoid, Malaria^, Y. Fever*
Sri Lanka	Hep. A, Polio, Typhoid, Malaria, Y. Fever*
Sudan	Hep. A, Polio, Typhoid, Malaria, Y. Fever*ʳ, Meningitis
Suriname	Hep. A, Polio, Typhoid, Malaria, Y. Fever*ʳ
Swaziland	Hep. A, Polio, Typhoid, Malaria, Y. Fever*
Syria	Hep. A, Polio, Typhoid, Malaria^, Y. Fever*

DIRECTORY

Tahiti	Hep. A, Polio, Typhoid, Y. Fever*
Taiwan	Hep. A, Polio, Typhoid, Y. Fever*
Tajikstan	Hep. A, Polio, Typhoid, Malaria^, Diphtheria
Tanzania	Hep. A, Polio, Typhoid, Malaria, Y. Fever*', Meningitis
Thailand	Hep. A, Polio, Typhoid, Malaria^, Y. Fever*
Togo	Hep. A, Polio, Typhoid, Malaria, Y. Fever**, Meningitis
Tonga	Hep. A, Polio, Typhoid, Y. Fever*
Trinidad and Tobago	Hep. A, Polio, Typhoid, Y. Fever*
Tunisia	Hep. A, Polio, Typhoid, Y. Fever*
Turkey	Hep. A, Polio, Typhoid, Malaria^
Turkmenistan	Hep. A, Polio, Typhoid, Y. Fever*, Diphtheria
Tuvalu	Hep. A, Polio, Typhoid, Y. Fever*
Uganda	Hep. A, Polio, Typhoid, Malaria, Y. Fever*', Meningitis
Ukraine	Hep. A, Polio, Typhoid, Diphtheria
United Arab Emirates	Hep. A, Polio, Typhoid, Malaria^
Uruguay	Hep. A, Polio, Typhoid
Uzbekistan	Hep. A, Polio, Typhoid
Vanatu	Hep. A, Polio, Typhoid, Malaria
Venezuela	Hep. A, Polio, Typhoid, Malaria, Y. Fever'
Vietnam	Hep. A, Polio, Typhoid, Malaria, Y. Fever*
Virgin Islands	Hep. A, Polio, Typhoid
Yemen	Hep. A, Polio, Typhoid, Malaria, Y. Fever*
Yugoslavia	Hep. A, Polio, Typhoid
Zaïre (DRC)	Hep. A, Polio, Typhoid, Malaria, Y. Fever**
Zambia	Hep. A, Polio, Typhoid, Malaria, Y. Fever'
Zimbabwe	Hep. A, Polio, Typhoid, Malaria, Y. Fever*

TO PUT THINGS IN PERSPECTIVE...

This chart details the percentage risk of infection for various diseases during a one month stay in a developing country.

Severe Diarrhoea	50.0%
Malaria (no tablets, visiting West Africa)	2.4%
Malaria (no tablets, visiting East Africa)	1.5%
Acute Respiratory Tract Infection	1.3%
Giardiasis infection	0.7%
Hospitalised abroad	0.4%
Hepatitis (all types)	0.4%
Amoeba	0.4%
Gonorrhoea	0.3%
Air evacuation	0.06%
Syphilis	0.04%
Typhoid fever (India, N., N.W. Africa)	0.03%
HIV infection	0.01%
Died abroad	0.001%
Cholera	0.0003%

Key

We have amalgamated the figures from the following references:
• Steffen, R. Lobel, H.O. *Travel Medicine* in Cook, G.C. (ed.) *Manson's Tropical Diseases* (20th edition, 1996, London).
• A survey of 7,886 Swiss travellers to developing countries. (Steffen, R. et al. *The Journal of Infectious Diseases* 1987; 156:1:84-91)
• A survey of 42,202 European tourists visiting tropical Africa. (Steffen, R. et al. *Bulletin of the World Health Organisation* 1990; 68 (3): 313-322)
• A review of 34 studies on travellers' diarrhoea. (Black, R.E. *Reviews of Infectious Diseases* 1990; 12: s73-s79)

ALTERNATIVE HEALTH ORGANISATIONS AND HERBAL STOCKISTS

The Society of Homoeopaths
2 Artisan Road
Northhampton
NN1 4HU
Tel: **01604-21400**

The Chinese Herbal Medicine Centre
34 Knight Hill
London
SE27 OHY
Tel: **0181-670 7477**

Herbline UK
Tel: **01323-834 803**
Open Tuesday, Wednesday, and Friday from 9-3.

Hambledon Herbs
Court Farm
Milverton
Somerset
TA4 1NS
Tel: **01823-401 205**
Cannot give advice over the telephone but they will send a mail order catalogue on request.

Neil's Yard Remedies
Hotline will answer any queries **0171-627 1949**
Mail Order:
Neil's Yard Remedies
31 King Street
Manchester
M26AA

Helios Homeopathic Pharmacy
97 Camden Road
Tunbridge Wells
Kent
TN1 2QR
Tel: **01892-536 393**

Further Reading:

The World Travellers Manual of Homoepathy by Dr. Colin B Lessell (£16.95, The C.W. Daniel Company)

A Handbook of Homeopathic Alternatives to Immunisation by Susan Curtis, (£5.99, Winter Press)

Prescription for Nutritional Healing by James F. Balch and Phyllis A Balch ($6.95, Avery Publishing Group)

NOTES ON CONTRIBUTORS

Jack Barker is a freelance travel writer and editor of the online *Travelmag* ezine.

Dr Nick Beeching is Senior Lecturer at the Liverpool School of Tropical Medicine, and is Clinical Director of the Infectious Disease Unit at Fazakerly Hospital in Liverpool. He and his young family have travelled widely and he has worked in India, Australia, New Zealand and the Middle East. He continues active teaching and research collaboration with colleagues in many parts of the tropics.

Col. John Blashford-Snell is founder of Operation Drake and Operation Raleigh, and fearless leader of countless expeditions world-wide.

Ingrid Cranfield is a freelance writer and broadcaster and has edited three earlier editions of *The Traveller's Handbook* (WEXAS).

Sheila Critchley is a Canadian journalist now based in London, and has run an airline in-flight magazine.

Adrian Furnham is a lecturer in psychology at London University. He is the co-author with Prof. F. Bochner of *Culture Shock: Psychological Consequences of Geographic Movement* (Methuen).

Miranda Haines is the editor of *Traveller* magazine and the 7th edition of *The Traveller's Handbook* (WEXAS). Previously she worked for the *International Herald Tribune* in Paris for two years before becoming a freelance journalist in London, specialising in travel and business journalism.

Richard Harrington is a widely travelled freelance travel writer.

Ian Irvine is a registered insurance broker, specialising in insurance for adventure and overland travellers.

Dr Saye Khoo of the Department of Infectious Diseases and Tropical Medicine at North Manchester General Hospital, was medical officer on the 1997 Malaysian Everest Expedition.

Julian McIntosh lived in Africa for several years, and has travelled extensively. His overland experiences prompted him to set up his own specialist tropical equipment firm.

Paul Pratt has been a ship's radio officer in the British Merchant Navy and an electronics engineer in Britain and Scandinavia.

Melissa Shales is a freelance travel writer and editor. She is also the editor of two previous editions of *The Traveller's Handbook* (WEXAS).

Sarah Thorowgood is a freelance editor and armchair traveller, and is the assistant editor of the 7th edition of *The Traveller's Handbook* (WEXAS).

Dr Sharon Welby is a lecturer in Travel Medicine at the Liverpool School of Tropical Medicine. She has worked in New Zealand, Malawi and Kenya, and has travelled widely.

FURTHER READING

World Travel Health Guide (**Columbus Press**)
Health Advice for Travellers (**Department of Health**)
Travellers' Health: How to Stay Healthy Abroad (**OUP**)
Stay Healthy Abroad: The essential guide for all travellers (**Health Education Authority**)
Centre for Disease Control's (CDC's) Guide to Healthy Travel (**Open Road Publishing**)
The Traveller's Handbook (**WEXAS**)
The World's Most Dangerous Places (**Fielding Travel Guides**)